TOUC[HING HEARTS,]
EDUCATING MINDS

To: Cheryl,

Keep the heart in

learning

Best Wishes

Richard S. Join

"A remarkable story, honestly told, full of accomplishment, pain, and promise—a hope that will not die." *-Dr. Parker Palmer*

TOUCHING HEARTS, EDUCATING MINDS

Story of a School with Soul & Determination

Richard L. Njus

TATE PUBLISHING & *Enterprises*

Published by Tate Publishing & Enterprises, LLC
127 E. Trade Center Terrace | Mustang, Oklahoma 73064 USA
1.888.361.9473 | www.tatepublishing.com

Tate Publishing is committed to excellence in the publishing industry. The company reflects the philosophy established by the founders, based on Psalm 68:11,
"The Lord gave the word and great was the company of those who published it."

Book design copyright © 2009 by Tate Publishing, LLC. All rights reserved.
Cover design by Lance Waldrop
Interior design by Blake Brasor

Published in the United States of America

ISBN: 978-1-60799-394-0
1. Education, Aims & Objectives
2. Education, Philosophy & Social Aspects
09.05.26

Dedicated to

Eleonora and Krisztina Njus,
My granddaughters.
May they be able to learn
in a place like Deerfield.

And

Gayle, my wife, whose love
and support have carried me
through our adventurous
life together.

Acknowledgments

"When your heart speaks, take good notes."

Judith Campbell

This book reflects the outcome of what happens when people put their heads and hearts together to create a special school. The experience of writing this book has been one of the most challenging and rewarding adventures of my career. I hope I took good notes of the many hearts that spoke in this book expressing what the experience of Deerfield Elementary School meant to them. I could not have done this without the caring support of many people and my Deerfield family.

To Dr. Emmett Lippe, Novi Community Schools Superintendent in 1999, and Dr. Rita Traynor, the Assistant Superintendent, for taking a chance on me and having faith in me to be the leader of the Deerfield project. Their support in creating and opening Deerfield was great. And thank you, Emmett, for telling me to follow my passion.

To each person who is named in this book, a special acknowledgment and thanks for the time you took to write down your thoughts about Deerfield. Your contributions are the essence of the Deerfield way. Your hearts spoke in a special way through the pages of this book. A special thanks to my Deerfield family for all your encouragement and support in writing this book. You showed a lot of faith in me to capture what we all experienced.

To the Deerfield staff, for your part in making the dream of Deerfield come true. Thank you for your heart for kids, for giving so deeply of yourselves to create our culture of care and learning. Thank you for all the extra effort you put into making miracles happen for your students. It has been a joy to work with you.

To the Deerfield students who so deeply touched my life and who are the culture of Deerfield, thank you for your daily smiles and hugs. The sharing of your joy and excitement for learning and the opportunity to share in your sorrows provided richness to my life, which can never be fully expressed. Thank you for helping me keep my perspective on life and letting me live out my passion. I love you too for making each day a great day to come to work.

To Dr. Eric Glover, I thank you for challenging me to write this book. If you had not, I never would have. I appreciate the leads for a publisher and guidance in writing. When you called after reading a draft and said it was powerful and a story that needed to be told, I could not have been more proud of my manuscript.

To Beth Dempsey, a former Deerfield parent and writer, my deepest gratitude for your enthusiastic support, insights, and motivation as I started the process of writing the story of Deerfield and for keeping me going. Thank you for your eternal optimism. To have a writer say I could write was such an encouragement. You helped me hone in on the theme of the book and to identify the heart of what needed to be expressed.

To Sherry Griesinger, one of the Deerfield teachers, who

knows my heart for Deerfield and has lived the Deerfield experience from the design of the program through the opening of the school and has taught in Deerfield to this day—I appreciate you volunteering to read, help, and give direction for clarification. You work miracles with kids in the classroom and helped your principal communicate the heart of our school.

To Dr. Parker Palmer, author of *The Courage to Teach*, my deepest thanks and gratitude for all you have meant to me in my life and vocation. My appreciation for taking time to read my manuscript and share your thoughts, give encouragement, and helpful direction.

To Alison Kroll, a Deerfield parent, for sharing her wonderful talents in editing and questions for revision to help communicate the heart of the Deerfield story. For your extraordinary assistance taking the time to read and reread the manuscript and to sit with me as we went through it page by page to make corrections. I can't thank you enough for your patience, insights, and phenomenal ability with words. You're a gem.

To Tate Publishing, my heartfelt gratitude to all who worked with me for being so kind, patient, and encouraging through the process of bringing my book to publication. Thanks to Donna Chumley, Rachael Sweeden, Lindsay Behrens, and the whole layout staff. A special thanks to Kalyn McAlister, my conceptual editor, who I felt truly understood the heart of my book and gave outstanding guidance in finalizing the manuscript. You were a joy to work with. My experience with Tate could not have been better. You made a dream come true.

To my family, my wonderful wife, your love and support has always been my mainstay. When you read a draft of my book and said that you could hear me on the pages, I knew then I had communicated from my heart. You are an incredible woman, and your love has made it possible for me to follow my heart. And to my sons, Jonathan and Jeffrey, thanks for your love and encouragement to keep writing my story. I appreciate some of your tough questions that made me dig deep into myself.

My deepest thanks to God, who gave me the love I have for children.

A special thanks to Fanning/Howey Associates, Inc., who designed Deerfield Elementary, for permission to use the designs and pictures in this book.

Table of Contents

Foreword 13

Introduction 17

Chapter 1   Touching Hearts and Lives 25

Chapter 2   Care, Connections, Passion 31

Chapter 3   Dream, Plan, Create. 37

Chapter 4   Bricks, Mortar, People 51

Chapter 5   The Process Begins 63

Chapter 6   Here We Come, Ready or Not. 75

Chapter 7   Parents as Partners 87

Chapter 8   Culture of Care and Learning 99

Chapter 9   Leadership 115

Chapter 10   Touching Hearts:
             More Deerfield Family Stories 127

Chapter 11   Prophecy Fulfilled, Dream Denied. . . 159

Chapter 12   Bitter or Better. 197

Chapter 13   Looking to the Future 209

Foreword

American education is facing many challenges, two of which are so serious that I call crises. The first crisis is the loss of purpose and the other the loss of faith. Richard Njus has written a book to address both. With a passionate account of his personal journey to create a school, he tells us the direction and restores our faith.

In his book *The End of Education: Redefining the Value of School*, the late cultural critic and New York University professor Neil Postman points out the importance of purpose and refers to it as "god," not the "God," but the reason for existence, the purpose for parents to send their children to school, the reason for children to stay in the classroom, and the reason for societies to have schools. As Postman says, "for schools to make sense, the young, the parents, and their teachers must have a god to serve, or even better, several gods. If they have none, school is pointless." (Postman, 1996, p. 4).

Recent education reforms exemplified by the No Child Left Behind Act (NCLB) have identified test scores and memorization of a standardized set of information as the god that schools should serve. As a result, school leaders, teachers, and the children are all forced to sacrifice themselves for this god. But this god is imposed by a few outsiders, the government, businesses, and the uninformed public.

This god is not the god for the teachers and students. The imposition of an external purpose not shared by the children and their teachers, who are the souls of education, essentially drove intrinsic purpose of education out of schools.

There are, of course, reasons for this imposition, according to the reform advocates. One of the most loudly touted reasons is that schools are supposed to provide a good education for all children, which is absolutely an indisputable mission. However, defining good education as good test scores takes us farther and farther away from what real good education is. Richard Njus helps to reclaim the purpose, the "god," of education. He reminds me of a wise counselor in ancient China who risked his life to change the mind of a king, who was apparently confused about purpose. This story was recorded in *Zhan Guo Ce* or the *Records of the Warring States*, a collection of essays about events and tales that took place during China's *Warring States Period* (475–221 BC). Here is my recount of the story.

The king of the state of *Wei* intends to attack its neighboring state of *Zhao*. Upon hearing the news, *Ji Liang*, counselor to the king rushes to see him. "Your Majesty, on my way here, I met a man on a chariot pointed to the north," *Ji Liang* tells the King, "and he told me that he was going to visit *Chu*."

"But *Chu* is in the south, why are you headed north?" I asked.

"Oh, no worry, my horses are very strong," he told me.

"But you should be headed south," I told him again.

"Not to worry, I have plenty of money," he was not concerned.

"But still you are headed the wrong direction," I pointed out yet again.

"I have hired a very skillful driver," was this man's reply.

"I worry, your majesty, that the better equipped this man was," *Ji Liang* says to the King, "the farther away he would be from his destination." "You want to be a great king and win respect from all people," *Ji Liang* concludes, "You can certainly rely on our strong nation and excellent army to invade *Zhao* and expand our territory. But I am afraid the more you use force, the farther away you will be from your wishes."

Richard Njus tells us that schools are supposed to "touch hearts and change minds" rather than producing standardized test takers. More importantly, Richard practices what he believes. I have been fortunate to see him practice his beliefs on many occasions and my own son was a direct beneficiary of his practices and beliefs. He has led the development of more than one school. Actually they are not schools, they are communities of learners, or havens for young souls.

Richard's experience at Deerfield Elementary, the very subject of this book, is a tale that helps address the second crisis in American education. NCLB and similarly spirited reforms basically pronounced the total loss of faith in public school educators. The reform strategies basically suggest that we no longer believe them. They have become complacent and lazy. They are coasting, holding low expectations of their students and themselves. Thus the government must come in, must hold them accountable, must make them compete, and must make their performances public. Their teaching must follow government censored standards, their work must be regulated, and their products must be evaluated with standardized testing.

Richard proves the reformers wrong. He and his colleagues are not complacent and lazy. They are creative, hardworking, and caring guardians of young hearts and minds. They are resolved to overcome difficulties and fight to preserve their gods—touching hearts and changing minds. They don't need externally imposed standards and accountability to motivate them because they are driven by an unstoppable internal desire to excel, to care, and to love.

Richard's tale is heroic, but with a taste of tragedy. It shows how difficult it can be to be innovative, to be true to your heart, and to keep the holy fire burning. The story of Deerfield Elementary, unfortunately serves as yet another example of Machiavelli's famous theory about change:

There is nothing more difficult to take in hand, more perilous to conduct, or more uncertain in its success, than to take the lead in the introduction of a new order of things. Because the innovator has for enemies all those who have done well under the old conditions, and lukewarm defenders in those who may do well under the new. (Machiavelli, 2006)

We need heroes. We need hope. We need faith. Education cannot be driven by fear of the past or the present, it must be inspired by hope for the future. And Richard Njus, in this book, gives that hope and faith. I thank him for having written this book.

Yong Zhao, Ph.D
University Distinguished Professor
Director, US-China Center for
Research on Educational Excellence
Director, Center for Teaching and Technology
Executive Director, Confucius Institute
College of Education
Michigan State University

Introduction

"Making connections among people,
establishing bonds of trust and understanding,
building community."

Better Together, by Robert d. Putnam
Lewis M. Feldstein

Touching Hearts, Educating Minds is a story about what happens when people put their hearts and heads together creating something very special, Deerfield Elementary School. A special thanks to Dr. Eric Glover, a professor from East Tennessee State University who challenged me to write this book about Deerfield Elementary School after hearing me share about it at a retreat. I had shared the experience I had had at Deerfield and the significant impact the school had on our students, staff, parents, the community, and me. Deerfield School became a school that truly challenged minds and touched hearts in a special way. We took the quote by Chief Sitting Bull to heart, "Let us put our minds together and see what life we can make for our children."

There is much debate in the U.S. and the world about education and what works. High-risk testing, No Child Left Behind, and grading schools are the latest trends. Are they the end all in making schools more proficient? I truly do not think so. I think the answer is in connections and culture within the school. It is not about books, programs, and curriculum. It is about people connecting, establishing trust, and understanding. It is about building a community of learners. It is the concepts quoted above from the book *Better Together*. This is what we experienced at Deerfield, and our test scores reflected our success.

Educational consultant Nancy Weber confirmed this in a presentation when she said, "A key finding in brain research is that the single most important factor in teaching is emotional connections." When I heard that statement, my mind began to spin with all the memories of experiences and conversations over the years on what is significant in teaching and learning. I have asked many parents what they want for their children in their school. It comes down to three things. They want their children to be safe, to be loved, and to learn to their potential. I share the wish of Rob Morrow, "That everyone has the opportunity to go to school in a safe, healthy environment where knowledgeable, passionate people help them learn the things that are important to be a citizen on this planet." This does not come through pressure, high-risk testing, or regulations. It comes through significant relationships. When I talk with adults about what the greatest effect was on their own learning, they don't say books, programs, classes, or forms of instruction; the significant experiences that people have had in learning are linked to a person or it is a person, personal connections, and culture.

Elizabeth Andrews says, "Good teaching comes not from behind the desk but from behind the heart." We have proven research on what is best in teaching and learning; those best

Richard L. Njus

practices that are so often talked about. We have model schools that are experiencing great success. We know what skills need to be taught. Yet we don't spend the time developing schools and the person who teaches those skills; the one who can take all the knowledge of learning and communicate it to his or her students. In my role as a principal for the past twenty-eight years in some very innovative schools, I have observed differences in successful schools and classrooms that ignited learning for students and those that just fulfilled the curriculum requirements. The key is passionate principals, teachers, and staff; people who have a passion for learning, the subject area they teach, and a love for children. Combine that with a strong partnership with parents, and a synergy for learning is created. Passion is contagious. People follow one who has passion. Passion ignites learning. Deerfield has been a journey reflected in a passionate culture for learning.

> What we teach will never take unless it connects with the inward, living core of our students' lives, with our students' inward teacher. . . . Good teachers possess a capacity for connectedness. The connections made by teachers are held not in their methods but in their hearts, and the more one loves teaching, the more heartbreaking it can be.
>
> Dr. Parker Palmer, *The Courage to Teach*

Children need to believe that the world is an interesting and safe place. The relationship between children and their teachers isn't incidental, but is the central component of their learning. Human development occurs within the context of real relationships. We learn from whom we love.

Mary Pipher, *The Shelter of Each Other*

Relationships, connections, love; this is what makes the difference in schools. It is the personality of the culture of the school. One can sense this in a school, feel it in the atmosphere, and see it in the eyes of students, teachers, and parents. This is the affective domain of a school. When this kind of culture is in place in conjunction with best practices in teaching and learning, schools experience success beyond their wildest dreams.

Our Deerfield staff has embraced the concept of the poster we have in our office with the quote by Forest E. Witcraft, "A hundred years from now, it will not matter what my bank account was, the sort of house I lived in or the kind of car I drove, but that the world may be different because I was important in the life of a child." Teachers and principals of passion make a difference and are important in their students' lives. Their connection with a child makes all the difference in the world.

The following pages are a journey in a caring community of learners. I will share how a school of quality connections and a deep culture is created; how when parents and staff put their heads and hearts together, they create something very special. I have visited many schools around the U.S. where this is happening. It can happen anywhere. Our journey in this book will take us through the creation of one school told through the stories and experiences by those who were a part of the Deerfield family. It is a story of a school with a rich soul and strong determination. It is my hope that as you read through these pages you will feel the soul of the school in the stories and experiences I share. Within the soul of Deerfield, you will see the determination of staff and parents to keep that special something when faced with resistance, criticism, and traditionalism. It happens so often in society when an organization, a person, or in our experience, a school is successful, tensions arise.

This is a story of the tremendous effort a staff and parents put into creating a magnet school only to be met with a business-as-usual mind set by their district board of education, attacks from other school families in the district, and misperceptions and misrepresentations of the school in the community. Yet, through all the frustration and anxiety, the staff and parents responded with a continuing sense of hope and an affirmation that nothing good can ever be lost. The e-mails and letters in this book communicate the rich effect of a school on students, parents, staff, and me. The stories give us a variety of perspectives on how a school can touch hearts and educate minds. Please join me on this incredible journey. May it affect and challenge you as it did me.

What can you say about a school that literally has changed our lives? Not nearly enough I imagine. I had originally enrolled my son, Jacob, at the Catholic school in Farmington that I attended. Two days into the school year, my husband, John, and I received a call from the principal. Turns out she had been the principal at the Catholic school in Redford that John attended as a child, she knew him well. We had a frank discussion, the bottom line being that the school simply could not provide the type of education that Jacob needed. He was (and still is!) extremely intelligent, and they simply could not provide the extra resources they felt he needed and deserved. They were aware that we lived in Novi, told us what a fantastic district it was, and suggested we enroll him in kindergarten there.

I was terrified. I had never set foot in a public school and couldn't imagine sending my son there. Jacob spent his first year at Orchard Hills. He was moved from classroom to classroom, first kindergarten, then a first/second-grade split class and finally to a second-grade room. The principal and teachers were nice, but in the end, it seemed they just did not know what to do with Jacob. At the end of the year, the principal suggested we enroll Jacob in the new school set to open in the fall—Deerfield. I still had doubt but didn't see any other option. Jacob started the year in a first/second-grade classroom. While the other kids were learning basic math and beginning to read, Jacob was interested in biology and the Earth's gravitational pull. I think the other children thought he was crazy; they simply had no idea what he was talking about. It was hard for Jacob to become friends with children that he could not relate to.

Jacob told me a story about walking into school one day with Mr. Njus. He was undoubtedly trying to usher Jacob into the school with the rest of the children. Jacob stopped to look at a puddle. Other principals would have taken Jacob by the arm and said, "Let's go." Mr. Njus stopped and asked him about what he saw, they talked about what was in the puddle, and then Mr. Njus walked Jacob to class. One thing was clear, Mr. Njus understood Jacob. Later, we met again with Mr. Njus, and he told us he wanted to move Jacob into Julie Kaufman's third/fourth-grade classroom. I was still a bit leery, having had Jacob in so many different classrooms the year before, and this would be moving up two grades. We had begun to trust Mr. Njus, so we agreed.

A day or so later, we met in a conference room—Jacob, Mr. Njus, Mrs. Kaufman, John and I. Mrs. Kaufman spoke directly to Jacob. She told him about her classroom, the rules and responsibilities. She talked about how above all, they respected each other. She was so genuine and her concern for him so apparent, that I almost cried. The children welcomed Jacob, but he was allowed to enter at his own pace. And shortly thereafter, finally, Jacob was in a class that he felt a part of. He spent the next three years there. The friendships that he made in that room continue to this day. There were bumps along the way, but it was always known that Mrs. Kaufman and Mr. Njus had Jacob's best interest at heart. Their patience and understanding is something I will always be thankful for.

There were, of course, other staff members that made incredible differences. At the time, I was working in Troy. If there was a problem, it took me a bit of time to get there, but I was comforted in knowing that Jacob was with people who truly cared about him. Mrs. Timreck in the office was unbelievably helpful, Ms. Sandy the intern was fabulous as was Mrs. Curly in the CARE program, and Ms. Wagner in the media center. Their kindness and concern will always be remembered.

When it came time for Jacob to move on, the staff at Deerfield was still offering help. Whether it was officially or unofficially, I could always count on Mrs. Kaufman and Mr. Njus to provide guidance, insight or just a sympathetic ear. Jacob left Deerfield in June of 2003, but I feel as comfortable calling them today as I did then. Although we have come across a few more truly amazing people in the Novi school system, most notably Dr. Ellis and Mr. Faletti, I am still amazed at the dedication of the staff at Deerfield. They have made an indelible difference in our lives, and for that I am truly grateful.

Stephanie, parent

Richard L. Njus

Chapter 1

Touching Hearts and Lives

"In life there are choices and chances.
Make a choice, take a chance,
reap the reward."

Anton, Better Together, pg 46

Why did I stop and look at worms with Jacob? What was my motivation? I should have been moving the kids along. I think I can explain this best by another story. This story is about an eight-year-old boy who was one of those kids that loved life and from the first day, liked going to school. Kindergarten, first, and second grade were great fun, he had a lot of friends, and he was loved by his teachers for his happy disposition. In the third grade, things began to change, and school became more difficult. He loved his teacher and tried to please her. He loved to learn; the problem was that he could not read. He could not make sense of letters and words. As the school year went on, his frustration level with learning increased.

Toward the end of third grade, the boy heard his mother talking at home on the telephone. It sounded like she was having a serious conversation with someone, so he listened in. He stood by the door to their study so he could hear yet not be seen. She was talking about school. Was she talking to his teacher? Was he in some kind of trouble? He could not think what he had done recently that would cause his teacher to call. It wasn't as if he never had gotten in trouble, but not enough for his teacher to call home.

Then his mother called to him to come see her. He went into the study. His mother said she and his teacher had been talking about how he was doing in school. She asked how he felt he was doing; was he having any problems? He said he was doing fine. Then he thought for a while, feeling guilty that he had not told the whole truth, and told her he was having a hard time reading. He shared how hard it was for him to figure out words. His mother said his teacher had called because she was concerned and wanted to talk with him about how he was doing in school. His mother asked him if he would talk with her.

The little boy took the telephone and nervously said hi. His teacher, with that caring tone in her voice, said she and his mother had been talking about how he was doing in school and asked him how he felt he was doing. He said okay, he guessed. He said he liked school. He wanted to make her feel good. She asked if he felt he was having trouble with anything in school. He said reading was hard. She talked with him about his struggle with reading and how they were working together. He knew he was having problems because he was in the non-readers group. His teacher also told him she knew he was smart and could learn to read. She said she had tested him and seen in his test scores that he had all the ability in the world. She said she believed in him and knew he could learn to read.

Richard L. Njus

They had a decision to make about next year. He could go to fourth grade with what he had learned knowing it would be a struggle. "Or," his teacher said, "you can stay another year with me. If you stay with me, I promise that I will help you to learn to read." His teacher said that his mother and she felt it was important to know how he felt in the decision. She said it really was his decision.

The little guy thought for a while about not moving on with his friends and what would they say. He would have to make new friends. It was hard to think about what he should do. He thought, *Why is it my decision?* He looked at his mother and then at the telephone, thinking about what his teacher said. Then he thought about how hard it was for him to read and keep up with his classmates. Most of all, he thought about what his teacher said. She believed in him and promised to help him learn to read. She said she knew he could be successful.

I am that little boy who made the decision to stay another year with Mrs. Rill, my third-grade teacher, and it made all the difference in the world for me. It changed the rest of my life. Because I stayed with Mrs. Rill, I have been able to go on and realize my potential.

As the quote says at the beginning of this chapter, "In life there are choices and chances. Make a choice, take a chance, reap the rewards." As a young boy, I took a chance and made a choice because I had a teacher and mother who believed in me. One of the most rewarding benefits of my choice is that it enables me to connect with the students who are having difficulty and some of the hard choices they have to make. But even more than that, I can give them understanding and hope.

Because of a teacher who loved me and with whom I connected, I was given a love and passion to share what she shared with me with students for the rest of my life. That is why I took the time to look at worms with Jacob. You see, she gave me a birthright for success. Because she believed in me no matter what anyone said or whatever the struggle, I knew I could be successful because she believed in me. It had nothing to do with the school, the books, or curriculum; my learning had everything to do with a culture of love. A culture that nurtured the possibilities of learning, not excuses for failure.

Because of Mrs. Rill I made it through school and went to college. I had some poor even down-right-mean teachers after Mrs. Rill, but because of her, I could keep faith in my possibilities. It was not easy. I had to work hard to make the grade all the way through high school. In fact, when I entered high school, my freshman counselor would not let me go into the college prep track when I told him I was going to go to college to be a teacher. He said my grades were not good enough. I was placed on the general education track. But Mrs. Rill said I could be successful. I did go to college and became a teacher. Then I went on to get my master's in educational leadership and found my vocation as a principal.

It is something that that little boy who "flunked" third grade made the dean's list in college. That one experience with a teacher I connected with is the torch I have carried through thirty-five years in education: to help all kids prove the world wrong when someone says they can't make it when learning is difficult, and to help all students realize their full potential. It helps me realize, as a principal, that culture is the key to success in a school. A successful school is one where teachers connect with their students to really make a difference. How is that culture of success developed? What is it that makes a school special and a place where each child can learn and grow as a whole child? How do you help children believe in themselves?

In the coming pages I want to share with you the story of Deerfield Elementary School, in Novi, Michigan, a school that truly made a difference in the lives of not only the students but the staff and the parents. It has made a tremendous difference in my life. I would like to thank all those who touched my life so richly through this experience. I would also like to thank Mrs. Rill for believing in me. I keep a picture of my third-grade class (my second year) in 1956 in my office to remind me of the legacy she gave me. I wish Mrs. Rill could have seen our school. I know she would have loved to walk through Deerfield with me and see all the students engaged in learning.

May you capture the depth of richness in culture that permeated the lives of those who were a part of the Deerfield experience. And may you take that to your school, put your heads and hearts together, and make your school a special place for children to learn and grow.

Dear Mr. Njus,
I don't know quite where to begin, so I guess it would be when David's name was drawn as one of the very lucky kids to be able to attend Deerfield for its first year.

With my kids' rough start in life, they received such a great deal of care and understanding from you and all the teachers, which they needed badly. I don't know what I could have done without the help that Mrs. Cingel and Mrs. Sherman have given me the past few years. They have been so generous with their time and thoughtfulness, both to the kids and me.

I don't know if you remember the challenge you had to keep Dana in her classroom and from not leaving the school property. She is doing so well now and loves school. I attribute that a great deal to the classroom structure and teaching methods and of course your watchful eye.

Please excuse this rough draft, as I am recovering from surgery on my arm and am just now able to write. (Wish I had as good penmanship as she does.)

I never enjoyed and laughed so much as during last years third- and fourth-grade stage production. They did such a wonderful job. Everyone; students, teachers, etc. should be proud of the job they did with such a challenging play as Pirates of Penzance; I didn't think David could handle it, but with all the support given, he sure did.

My kids having such an "older mom" is difficult for them, I know and am so grateful they are and were able to go to Deerfield.

Thank you so much "everyone."

Sincerely,

Melva Parsons, parent

Chapter 2

Care, Connections, Passion

"Where the passion of your heart meets
the needs of the world this is your joy."

Frederick Bueckner

The little boy grew up, and his heart carried the confidence
and love for learning ignited in him by Mrs. Rill, his third-
grade teacher. At sixty-two I have had a life filled with the
blessings of working with children, parents, and staff sharing
that love of learning instilled in me by her. In the book *And
You Know You Should Be Glad* by Bob Greene, he says, "Life,
when you let it, can thrill you." That is so true. It has been
a wonderful thrill seeing children prove the world wrong,
perform beyond expectations, and be a part of schools which
performed beyond belief.

My career has taken me from a classroom teacher in sixth
and second grade to principal of four elementary schools. I
have had the privilege of working with outstanding creative
teachers, with their passion to provide the best opportunities
in learning for kids, to develop programs and school cultures
that reaped great results. Our schools were highly successful
in the school community.

In my first principalship in Paw Paw, Michigan, which I
took with excitement and fear, I quickly discovered the won-

derful things that happen when people put their heads and hearts together. In a short period of time, we went from a school that did not welcome parent involvement to a school with more than two hundred parents volunteering each week and a grandparent program with twenty-five to forty seniors volunteering in our program each Thursday afternoon for two hours. We were the first school in the area to have a computer in every classroom (commodore 64s). We were the only school in the county to have a kindergarten-through-fifth-grade Spanish program. The success of our school and programs were noted throughout the area and state.

My second and third principalships were in Okemos, Michigan, near Lansing. For six years I was the principal of the oldest school in the district. We experienced great success in developing a rich culture for learning as reflected in our motto, "Where learning and caring equal excellence."

In 1991, I was asked to open a new elementary school in the fall of 1992. What a great experience. We not only had a beautiful award winning building to work in, but more importantly, we had a great staff of high performers to open the school. Opening a school is very attractive to high energy, high achieving, and talented teachers. It is an intensive, emotionally taxing yet exhilarating experience. Opening this school was yet another experience of a community putting their heads and hearts together, creating something very special. We created a great culture for learning. Total strangers would comment on feeling something special when they entered the school.

A few of our accomplishments were implementing an alternative/year-round calendar. We became a school of choice for the district. We developed a close partnership with Michigan State University, which helped us integrate a high level of technology into our instructional program. Michigan State also provided interns (full-year student teachers) for all classrooms. This also led to the development of many innovative programs. Our school became a site where many educators came to observe and study innovative education in practice. But the greatest success was a caring culture for learners where students realized their potential.

Let us now start our journey together in the story of a school with soul and determination.

Before attending third grade at Deerfield Elementary, our son, Tony, attended another school in the district from developmental kindergarten through second grade. Tony has a late November birthday, and because of that, we chose to enroll him in the developmental kindergarten class. Tony had a wonderful year in developmental kindergarten and appeared to be progressing as expected-emotionally and mentally. In the third week of his kindergarten year, we were very surprised when we were contacted by his teacher. She had decided based on the three-week school year to label him, which led to a steady decline in his self-confidence. At first, the school wanted to address the issue without our help or involvement. When we expressed concern and disappointment about our lack of involvement, the school then became very determined that we address the issue their way. We tried very hard to address the school's issues and concerns and still do what we felt was right for our son, but nothing appeared to satisfy them.

By second grade, it was very evident to us that the label had taken on its own persona and perpetuated to a point where it was not possible for Tony to be viewed in any other light. The entire focus of his second-grade year was the label and not the academics. When we challenged the school on their lack of focus towards Tony's academics, the school took no accountability and placed all of the blame on our shoulders and our son's.

The whole experience took a heavy toll on our family and especially on Tony who had a very negative perception of school and himself academically. This concerned us greatly. We decided it was time to explore other options. We heard about Deerfield in the community, but really had no understanding of what they offered in comparison to a neighborhood school. We went on the Deerfield tour and really liked the idea of the alternative teaching philosophy. Within the first week at Deerfield, Tony's teacher took us aside and assured us that Tony was not the label that he had been given previously. She did inform us that he was behind academically and the focus finally became about his academics. In a very short period of time, Tony has made huge strides academically. More importantly, with the help of his teachers, he is repairing his badly bruised self-esteem and confidence. For the first time since we became a part of the Novi School District, we feel like our kids are in a nurturing and caring environment. The teachers truly care about the welfare of our children.

What we personally learned from this experience is that some children do not fit into the traditional style of schooling and for those who do not, we have to offer alternatives. Deerfield is just the start of those alternatives. Although the decision to make Deerfield another neighborhood school saddens us for our own personal reasons, it also saddens us for those children who will suffer the same fate as our son.

Anna, parent

Chapter 3

Dream, Plan, Create

"Whatever you do, you need courage. Whatever course you decide upon, there is always someone to tell you that you are wrong. There are always difficulties arising that tempt you to believe your critics are right.

To map out a course of action and follow it to an end requires some of the same courage that a soldier needs.

Peace has its victories, but it takes brave men and women to win them."

Ralph Waldo Emerson

I remember the day in the spring of 1999 when I received the call offering me the position to be the principal of a magnet school to open in the fall of 2000. The call came at 4:37 p.m. on a Wednesday after my seventh interview of two hours and weeks of interviews for the position. My wife, Gayle's comment was, "You know, Richard, you have been marching to the beat of a different drum your whole life, and now you have finally gotten a job at a place that is playing your tune." How true it was. The job description was everything I had dreamed about doing in a school. I finally could work in a school district that was forward thinking, researching and seeking out what is best for students in teaching and learning. After extensive research, they were willing to take the risk to create a school they saw most appropriate for learners. It would be a great challenge and a privilege to be a part of such a trail-blazing endeavor. The school was to set the tone for change and development for the whole district's elementary system.

I took the leap of faith and accepted the position. I would be going from a five-minute to an hour drive to work to pursue a dream. I think I can sum up how I felt through our Deerfield experience by using a quote from the book *The Zanzibar Chest* by Aiden Hartley. He quoted Eric Ransdell who said,

> I've never had a time like that since, when what I wanted to be doing with my life and the life I was living, were so utterly intertwined. And I'm old enough now to understand that most people never get anything close to that in the course of their lives. Nor have I ever cared so much about what I was doing.

What a journey it has been, this experience called Deerfield. Before I go into more personal experiences with the journey of the magnet school, I would like to begin with the background on the process of Deerfield's development.

The story of Deerfield Elementary school began with the Innovative Elementary School Cadre, a committee to design and research best practices for the development of a new school. The cadre was made up of twelve parents, six teachers and staff, one community-at-large member, four administrators, and one board member. In the summer of

1997, the administration appointed a facilitator and the director of curriculum to facilitate a committee or cadre, which would research best practices for the design of an innovative approach to K-4 elementary education in the Novi Community School District in Novi, Michigan. This is an upper-middle-class school district about thirty minutes from Detroit and Ann Arbor.

The cadre met throughout the year, no consideration ever was given to facility; rather the sole intent of the members was to envision an innovative elementary-based program and to provide a framework for that vision. Some of the assumptions that the cadre made were: the school program would be provided in a safe and orderly climate for learning; there would be sufficient attention given to the selection of the teaching and administrative staff; selection and training of staff would be well designed; program implementation would be monitored and adjusted.

The cadre met eleven times during the year. They had four opportunities to visit Michigan schools that had innovative approaches to programming. The cadre did extensive research for the project. They based their work and research on answering the following questions:

1. How do people learn?
2. What should be learned?
3. How should learning be designed?
4. How will we know if learning occurs?
5. How should schools be designed to accommodate the desired learning?

Each cadre member selected a topic of interest from the five previous questions, and from that, five study groups were formed. Each group was provided with packets of research materials to study. The groups met to discuss, share, and analyze the main points of the topic, which they felt were strong concepts toward the final vision for an innovative learning and teaching climate.

The information and the selected decisions on the study were organized into group presentations and videotaped. A process was used that encouraged consistent interaction within the cadre between presenters and listeners. The presenters and listeners deepened their understanding and commitment to how students should learn and what essential elements of program design would improve student competencies and joy of learning.

The final recommendations of the cadre for what an innovative elementary program could be like for the school district was based on an accumulated knowledge of best practices and research. The cadre envisioned that all students would be consistently involved in:

- teaching and learning interactive opportunities to enhance academic strengths and skills, interests, and needs.

- integrated curriculum experiences

- studying topics in depth

- participating in foreign language studies

- gaining an understanding of global education

Richard L. Njus

by consistent use of interactive
media and technology

- maintaining a relationship with teachers
  over a prolonged period of time

- performances, i.e., demonstrating in front
  of their peers, teachers, and parents
  what they know and are able to do

- sustaining a three-way commitment through an
  individual performance contract between
  themselves, their teacher, and their parent.

- extended academic learning experiences
  at various times of the year

The cadre finalized their work with the following vision: "A program where schooling meets the learning styles, interests, and needs of *all* children with parents and staff committed to ensuring a variety of opportunities for children to acquire and to demonstrate what they know and are able to do."

The following diagram gives a breakdown of the process of the cadre and the research used. It shows the extent at which the cadre went to develop a school that truly meets the needs of all students with proven practices.

INNOVATIVE ELEMENTARY
RESEARCH GRAPHIC ORGANIZER

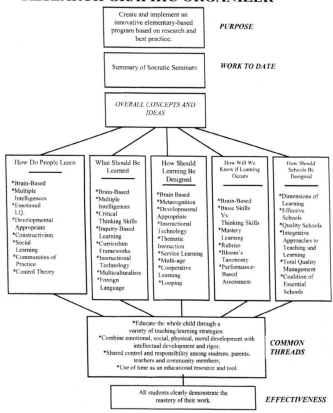

The lists below show the differences between the traditional schools and the innovative school. This is information we used to help staff and parents gain a clear understanding of the concepts for the school prior to opening and how it differed from a traditional school.

Richard L. Njus

New Elementary Program	Existing Elementary Program
At the Innovative Elementary Building, all students, all staff would consistently be involved in:	Presently, within the Novi Elementary Program some teachers are:
- teaching and learning opportunities to enhance their strengths and interests	- working independently on this concept
- integrated curriculum practices	- working independently on this concept
- studying topics of interest in depth	- working independently on this concept
- foreign language instruction	- there is no program
- becoming more aware of global education	- applying the new Social Studies Standards to a global perspective
- teamed by interests, academic strengths, and needs	- working in teams on this concept
- developing a long-term relationship with teachers	- working in teams on this concept
- developing a three-way commitment between parents, children, and teaching teams	- there is no established practice at this time
- demonstrating what they know and are able to do	- working in teams on this concept
- doing research at their Classroom Multi-Media Technology Center	- there is no Classroom Multi-Media Technology Center
- extended academic learning experiences before, after, or during school breaks	- there is no academic program at this time

The school board accepted the recommendation of the cadre for the innovative program to be used in the new elementary school to be built. They chose to create an elementary school where everyone was in the school by choice—students and staff. This was to preserve the purity of the program. The school board then hired an architectural firm to design the school. Rather than designing a school from plans they had used for other schools and alter the design for Deerfield, they developed the plans for the school to facilitate the program. They spent time with staff and administration in defining the correct design for the school. They looked at the need for space and light, taking into account the latest brain research.

Formation of the classrooms into K-4-grade houses with the ability of having flow for grouping and regrouping of students was very important. The K-4 houses were built in response to the research on the effect of students staying with a teacher for more than one year and the significant effect on learning. If a child would enter Deerfield in kindergarten, he or she would know the five teachers in their house for five years. Students knowing their teachers for multiple years provides for a smooth transition, and there is no time lost each fall for staff and students to get to know each other. With whole house activities, the upper- and lower-grade-level students would have a significant relationship with all teachers in their house.

The cadre wanted areas in each house for whole house activities. The need for teacher work areas and coatrooms for students was also taken into consideration. They created the library/media center to be a flexible learning area for multi functional learning activities. There was an attempt to use the surrounding area of the school for learning; from an amphitheater, tables, and benches in the courtyard for students to use in their learning to a wetland that they wanted to integrate into the learning environment. The committee went to great lengths to make every aspect of the building and the site learner-friendly and conducive to the facilitation of the program the cadre developed.

Below are footprints of the school architectural firm of Fanning/Howey Associates designed and built. One can see the flow from the houses to the specials' classrooms, cafeteria, stage, and to the outside learning areas. In the development of the school, we created four K-4 multi-age (houses) in two wings with room for students to work in flexible groups.

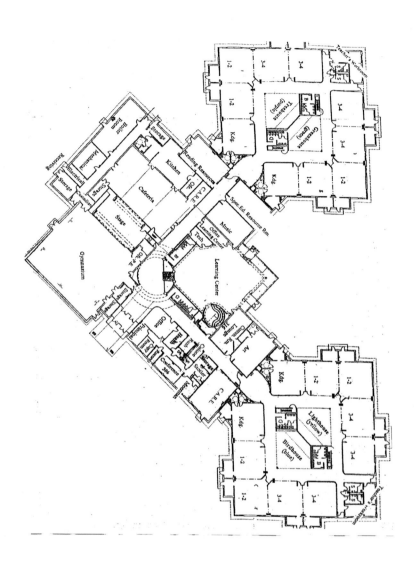

The next footprint depicts one of the four houses, made up of a full-day kindergarten classroom, two first/second multi-age classrooms, and two third/fourth-grade multi-age classrooms with an adjoining project area. This enables grouping and regrouping throughout the day to meet each student's needs. It creates a flow for learning.

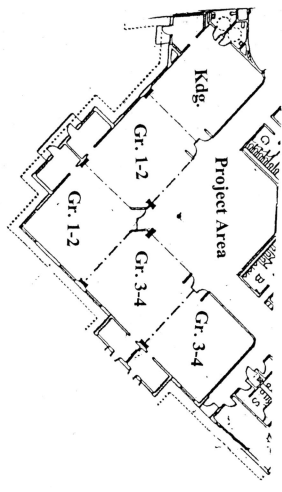

Each house took on its own personality. We had the Bird House, Tree House, Light House, and Green House. The names were decided by the staff. Each house is also designated by a color. Moveable walls were designed in the building to enable students to move from room to room and flow into a project area for a variety of learning experiences. The architect, Fanning/Howey Associates, Inc., did a wonderful job in designing a school that facilitates our program. As they describe the school in one of their pamphlets,

> *Deerfield Elementary School is a 500-student facility that supports a multi-age learning approach in two multi-age neighborhoods. The design offers a compelling connection between the building and its heavily wooded site, celebrating the environment and utilizing the outdoors as a center of learning. The school's vibrant media center and lobby bring the outdoors in with a colorful diorama depicting a woodland setting; an illuminated domed ceiling depicting the sky, greenhouse, planetarium; acoustical murals representing the seasons, and an engaging carpet graphics reflecting the globe and phases of the sun.*

In 2002, Deerfield won the prestigious Shirley Cooper Award: the top national school design award from the American Association of School Administrators (AASA) for the school design that facilitates the program most effectively. The school was also awarded the AS&U's Crow Island School Citation, the top award for educational interiors, and the William W Caudill Citations, AS&U's top annual award for school design. Awards are great, but as I said to our school board, "If we are not doing what we should for the students in the school, we should bulldoze the school down."

Do you know why the school was named Deerfield? Well, it started when the school was being built. Almost every day that the construction workers came to work on the school, there was a family of beautiful white-tailed deer that walked in the open field next to the school. Then, when the school was done, everyone got to vote on the school's name. They decided to stick to the wildlife theme, you know, Parkview, Village Oaks, Novi Woods, and Orchard Hills. Then some one heard about the story of the deer and said, "Deerfield." The name stuck and has ever since. It is an awesome school, and when you first walk in, there is an exhibit of wildlife you see around the school and the white-tailed deer is there!

Dominique, former Deerfield student

At Deerfield we are polite, caring, responsible, and we respect one another. We are multi-aged. We are in houses. That means we can know more people and make more friends. In each house we don't just have one grade. We have a combination of kindergarten, first, second, third, and fourth grade in one house. There are four houses and they have different names for them. They are Green House, Tree House, Bird House, and Light House. Our principal's name is Mr. Njus. He is a very nice man. We go to him for help when we have problems. Deerfield is a very happy and special place.

You should come to this school too!

Mitchel, second grade

Chapter 4

Bricks, Mortar, People

"The Basic School is about helping each child
build a life as if it were a work of Art."
                          Dr. Ernest Boyer

In 1999 they began the construction of the school. I was hired
for the 1999–2000 school year to work with the contractors
and to sell the concept of the school to the community and
throughout the school district. I was also responsible for the
hiring and training of staff and the facilitating of program
development. During that first school year, I worked daily
with the contractors revising plans and then monitored the
building of the school.

I worked in the finalization of the program with the
assistance of our school district assistant superintendent, Dr.
Rita Traynor. In the development of the program, we worked
with the cadre proposal, studied research, and visited schools
around the country to gather more ideas and information to
help us refine our philosophy and the program. We visited
schools throughout Michigan and the mid-west that had
multi-age classrooms, were magnet schools for their district,
and had special programs of interest. We visited Lincoln
School in Mundelein, Illinois, which was a magnet elementary school built on best practices in teaching and learn-

ing; the Key School, a K-12 magnet school in Indianapolis, Indiana, built with the help of Dr. Howard Gardner on Multiple Intelligences with many of the attributes we were interested in for our school; Huntington Woods Elementary School in Wyoming, Michigan, which was a magnet school built on the framework of Dr. William Glasser's Quality School; Birmingham Covington School in Birmingham, Michigan, a sixth-through-eighth-grade multi-age magnet school; Basic Schools in Kansas City, Kansas; and many other schools in Michigan with specific programs of interest. These visits were very helpful in the development and initiation of our program. The attributes of our school, which we established, were:

- Multi-age houses: K-4 students
  working and learning together
- Instruction and projects with themes
- Grouping of students to meet their learning needs
- Full-day kindergarten
- Common curriculum themes throughout the school
- Quarterly reports (students, parents, teachers)
  student-led conferences
- Variety of assessment instruments,
  including portfolios
- Parent involvement: volunteers, resources,
  enrichment, support
- Art, music, physical education/movement,
  integrated into the basic curriculum
- Spanish
- Consistent use of interactive media and
  technology to enhance all curriculum areas

We chose the Basic School framework program for our school. The Basic School was developed through Ernest Boyer and the Carnegie Foundation for the Advancement of Teaching. The Carnegie Foundation sponsored a twenty-five-year study of the basic or lower school and the early learner. They compiled the outcome of their research of best practices of teaching and learning in the book *The Basic School* by Dr. Ernest L. Boyer. Best practices are not just a practice that works in one school, they are practices that work over time in many schools in varied environments.

In 1999 our district assistant superintendent, Dr. Rita Traynor, and I attended a Basic School conference in Kansas City, Kansas. It was very helpful in developing our training and programming for the opening of the school. We also received help and support from the Basic School personnel through the process of opening the school. They provided materials, training, and technical support that helped us to successfully get the concepts of the Basic School off the ground with staff and parents. The basic school regional director, Dr. Gus Jacob, came to Michigan and spoke to teachers and parents about Basic School research and how it applied to Deerfield. It was very helpful in the process of informing our community about the program of our school and a great help for parents to know that this program was (and still is) working in other places throughout the United States. We also stressed in our program and in discussions with parents and staff Dr. Howard Gardener's work on Multiple Intelligences and Dr. William Glasser's concept on quality schools.

The vision for the school was clear. Deerfield would provide a program where schooling meets the learning style, interests, and learning stages of all students, and where parents and staff are committed to ensuring a variety of opportunities for our children to acquire and to demonstrate what they know and are able to do. Deerfield School incorporates the community's goals for children with sound, innovative, and effective educational concepts. The staff developed our mission statement as: "the joy of learning." When students feel the joy of learning, they are highly motivated to learn. The motto we chose and tried to live out for our school is "a caring community of learners." The caring aspects of learning for the whole child would be stressed through service learning activities. Character development would be integrated throughout our curriculum. Caring is modeled and taught. Nelson Mandela said, "No one is born hating another person because of the color of his skin, or background, or religion. If (people) can learn to hate they can be taught to love, for love comes more naturally to the human heart than its opposite." This is reflected in the quote we placed on the wall of our office: "Where love is deep, much can be accomplished."

In teaching to the whole child, one is filling not only the brain with knowledge, but also the heart with love. Our love and care nurtures the whole student. It gives them the support to take risks and learn. It also models the attributes of love we are trying to teach our students, which will fulfill their lives. This was experienced through the yearly service learning activities we provided for our students to help them realize the joy of giving and sharing. We raised funds to give both locally, nationally, and internationally. We taught and encouraged our students through yearly clothing drives, donations of candy after Halloween for senior citizens, and donations to "Paws for a Cause." Internationally we raised over one thousand dollars to partner with our local Rotary Club to build homes destroyed by the earthquake in India, raised money for tsunami relief, and raised more than two thousand dollars for an African orphanage for those who lost parents from AIDS. We have partnered with our local high school to raise funds for families touched by cancer. In 2007, we raised more than fifteen thousand dollars for St. Jude's Children's Hospital and over eleven thousand dollars for Juvenile Diabetes.

As part of the development of our program, we developed the following belief statement for Deerfield:

We believe:

- in a safe, secure, caring environment for learning;
- in the development of the whole child;
- in respect for self and others;
- everyone can learn and contribute;
- learning occurs in a variety of ways;
- teachers are facilitators of learning;
- parents are partners in learning;
- character is a valuable component of education.

We took the Basic School four priorities of community, curriculum, climate, and character as a framework of communicating the program and purpose for Deerfield. It was very helpful in putting our program in an understandable framework for parents and staff. Following are the four priorities with a brief description of each.

The school as Community

A Shared Vision: Deerfield is a place where staff, students, and parents come together to promote learning, with all classrooms connected by a clear and vital mission.

Teachers as Leaders: Teachers are leaders, who work together in teams and serve as inspired mentors to their students, encouraging them to become self-motivated learners. Our principal is considered the lead teacher.

Parents as Partners: The circle of our community embraces parents as the child's first and most important teacher.

A Curriculum with coherence

Centrality of Language: Knowing that literacy is the first and most essential goal, all children are expected to become proficient in the written and spoken word, as in mathematics and the arts.

Core Curriculum: Teachers use the district's core curriculum content standards. Students study various fields of knowledge through themes and projects. Instruction is designed to meet the learning styles, interests, and learning stages of students.

Measuring Results: A variety of assessments are used, including portfolios. Staff will report quarterly to parents, with student led conferences held at least twice yearly.

A Climate for Learning

Patterns to Fit Purpose: Every student is encouraged to become a disciplined, creative, self-motivated learner. Students are grouped in many different ways: multi-age groups, small groups, whole class groups, and interest groups. Individual student needs are continually being assessed.

Resources to Enrich: A multitude of resources for learning—from building blocks to books to computers—are available to all students.

Support Services for Children: The staff is committed to servicing the whole child. Beyond a solid academic program, our staff provides support, remediation, and enrichment programs.

A Commitment to Character

Character Building: Attributes of character are integrated into our instruction and program. The seven traits—*honesty, respect, responsibility, compassion, self-discipline, perseverance,* and *giving*—are emphasized to guide the school as it promotes excellence in living as well as learning.

Living with Purpose: Character is taught by both work and deed. Through curriculum, school climate, and service, students are encouraged to apply the lessons of the classroom to the world around them.

These attributes of the Basic School were used over and over in the meetings with parents and staff to give a clear understanding of the school. When the school opened, we posted the priorities in the entryway with the caption above them: Deerfield Elementary School serving children through the four priorities of the Basic School, along with a quote from Ernest Boyer, "The Basic School is about helping each child build a life as if it were a work of art." When the school opened, it helped to communicate to all who entered what our philosophy was. After hiring staff, we used the book *The Basic School* by Dr. Ernest Boyer for a staff book study to provide all staff with a deeper understanding of best practices in teaching and learning and those that specifically applied to our school.

> Wow, where does one start. I remember back when Deerfield was being built. Mr. Njus was holding meetings for parents to attend and learn about this new school and the philosophy behind it. Being an educator myself as well as coming from a family of educators, I was quite skeptical. As I listened to Mr. Njus, I must say that I did buy into his system. I believe that each child is a unique individual and has their own learning styles. I was familiar with Howard Gardner's Multiple Intelligences and knew that to bring out the best in each child you need to figure out where their strengths and weaknesses lie. However, I was also a realist. Having taught for many years, I knew that public schools were overcrowded and the curriculum wasn't always developmentally appropriate.
>
> Mr. Njus had wonderful ideas, but did he have the backing and the possibility of actually carrying out

this philosophy? I wasn't sure, and I sure didn't want my child to be a guinea pig. In my eyes, first grade is the most important grade, and I didn't think I could afford to make the wrong choice. So I didn't move my child. But I waited and I watched and I listened.

Two years later, when it was time for my daughter to begin her educational career, I went to Deerfield in February for the required "tour" with Mr. Njus. What I saw on that tour has changed me forever. As we walked around the school (the children were in session), I was totally in awe. There was a quiet hum around the school and everywhere we went we saw children actively engaged in learning. There were no doors to open and you couldn't tell one classroom from the next. The children did not become distracted by a group of twenty-five parents walking around and talking among themselves. We saw children working in small groups without adult intervention, teachers teaching a lesson to large or small groups, bigger kids seemed to be helping younger ones and everywhere you looked there was some type of learning going on.

My favorite memory of that day was while we were waiting for Mr. Njus to start the tour. Approximately three or four classes walked by us and the children were walking quietly but some of them were reading books and sharing it with others in line. They would read a passage, point to a picture, and laugh together or discuss it quietly. I've never seen anything like it in any school hallway I've been in. The children had seemed to take responsibility for their own learning.

How on earth had this happened? I wasn't sure, but I knew that I wanted my children to be a part of it. As Mr. Njus ended the tour with a recap of his philosophy; he said something to the effect of "This is what I believe and I want you to believe it too. If you don't, that's okay; Novi has terrific schools, and if you don't think this is the place for you then I'm sure your home school will be a better fit." Wow! To even have the luxury to be able to say that! Anyway, after a few hitches (we were number 110 in the lottery drawing), both of my children did end up getting to be students at Deerfield Elementary and I've never looked back.

Since I job-share my teaching position in my own district, I have had the advantage of being able to be a parent volunteer. This has been an invaluable experience for both me and my children. Each "house" in Deerfield truly is its own family. The children have the advantage of working at their own level and with others who may be a different age yet are also working at that level. For holiday parties, (in our "house"), each teacher plans a center in his/her room and then all 125 children have the option of visiting the centers of interest to them. You would think that this would be pure chaos, but because the teachers and children all know each other, it just seems to work out.

On Fridays the children do math centers this way as well. Each teacher plans a few centers around the theme that week and gears it for different levels. When a child comes to the center, they can pick which level meets their needs. There are teachers, parent volunteers, and other students that can help out if the need arises. The children know this and seem very comfortable taking risks and challenging themselves.

The children also do family groups with their own siblings as well as another family or two with their siblings. They will do a project or an activity together. The children eat in the lunchroom and have lunch recess with their "house." All these things have really brought my children closer together, not only with themselves but with others. They don't look at other children now just as being a third grader but as a person who might be good at math or needs extra help with scissors. I feel that they have learned to respect themselves, others, and adults in ways that are beyond their years. School has become an extension of our home and there is no longer the fear of the following school year, new teachers or new friends. It encompasses their whole being, and it's who they are. The Deerfield pledge says it all.

Forgive me, Mr. Njus, for doubting what you, your staff, and the people of Novi could do. My family and many others have truly been blessed by being a part of this Deerfield Community.

Beth DesOrmeau, Deerfield parent since
2002, Michigan teacher since 1987

Chapter 5

The Process Begins

"Your passion for your new work will eventually overwhelm your fear of letting go of your old source of stability."

Steve Pavlina

There were many activities and meetings leading up to the opening of the school. September 1999 through March of 2000, I met with all school personnel at their building staff meetings about the school and answered questions about the concept and programs for the school. Mostly staff of the other buildings in the district wanted to know the impact of Deerfield's program on their school. I remember at one staff meeting at the end of my presentation a teacher in the back of the room asked, "Is this going to cause us to change?" My response was, "I hope so, because we all continually need to look for what is best for students and should be in a process of continual change." I always encouraged staff who had questions to talk with me. I had an open-door policy for staff to talk about the school, especially for staff interested in coming to teach at Deerfield. I had a number of staff with whom I spent hours in discussion about the school and their dreams about teaching and learning. It was a great opportunity to meet potential staff and get to know them.

I conducted fourteen meetings for parents from August of 1999 to February of 2000 to share with them the concepts of Deerfield. I shared the design of the building and the program of the school. We talked about the different attributes of the school in comparison to a traditional school. We used many of the materials developed by the cadre to define and clarify the school and its differences from a traditional school. We tried at each meeting to paint a clear picture of what Deerfield would be like. I used many handouts showing the differences from a traditional school in the different programs: full day kindergarten, multi-age grouping, Spanish, character program, teaming, and the overall building philosophy and design. I fielded many questions on each facet of the program. Major issues were about multi-age grouping of students, full-day kindergarten, Spanish, thematic instruction, and the set up of the houses. I spent a lot of time fielding questions trying to clarify and help parents have a good understanding of the school. This was the time we started the process of connecting with our future parents; the process of building the Deerfield community. We tried to be open and honest, to be good listeners, and to gain parents' trust.

I sat down with many parents in my office to discuss the program. There was a feeling that this was something new and those attending were going to be guinea pigs. I helped them understand that the concepts used in the school were tried and proven over time: best practices. Parents wanted to know how this multi-age classroom would work. Would their child be challenged? Would older students teach younger students? What are the benefits? I shared that multi-age breaks down the concept of teaching a grade level or grade curriculum and puts the emphasis on teaching the child. We taught on what we called a continuous progress model, where students learn at their own rate and pace. There was no ceiling for learning. One doesn't stop learning at grade level; one is encouraged to go as far as he or she can. Parents and I talked at length about this. It was hard for parents to understand because it wasn't the way their school was when they were learning. I would laugh about this with parents and show them the picture in my office of me in the third grade where the desks were still connected. I could empathize with them that this was very different from the way I learned too. The experience was enriching and a tremendous time of learning for me. It was interesting to observe the change in peoples' concepts of the school as they gained a better understanding of the program and the research that backed it up. This process also helped me attain a deeper understanding of our school and program. It goes with the saying that the best learning comes through teaching.

In March of 2000 we began to receive applications for students of parents interested in sending their child to the school. We had an overwhelming response. In fact we had to have a lottery to fill the one hundred student spaces in full-day kindergarten classrooms because we had so many who were interested in coming. We had eighty on the waiting list for kindergarten the first year. The charge I had received from my superintendent in 1999 was that I had to have three hundred and fifty students to keep Deerfield a magnet/school of choice status. The lottery for the school was held in April. We had four hundred and fifty students for the opening of our school in August of 2000. We exceeded our goal by one hundred students.

After the April lottery, I sent welcome letters to the parents of the students attending. I had parents' meetings and began sending monthly newsletters about the progress of the school. I also established our Deerfield Community Council (parent group) board. We chose a council rather than a PTO or PTA because we wanted the parents to feel their influence as an advisory board not just a parent support group. It went along with our philosophy of parents as partners. I asked parents from each of the four feeder schools to be on the board. That was very helpful in the transition and in bringing the families together. I also met with students at each of the feeder schools who would be attending Deerfield in the spring before they went home for the summer. I showed them pictures of the plans for the school and encouraged them to go by and see it as it was being built.

For the hiring of staff, we posted positions in March of 2000 for the upcoming year. I had a meeting for teachers from within the district who had interest in coming to Deerfield. The meeting was supposed to last two hours. We had over sixty teachers in attendance. I shared the concepts of the school and the expectations for the teachers who wished to come and be a part of opening the school. I answered many questions pertaining to the philosophy and program of the school. They wanted to know about teaming and how I was going to assign teams and what kind of training they would receive. What really interested me was that the staff questions were not as much about the school, but about who I was as the principal. It taught me a lesson. These teachers were more interested in who they were going to follow than with what they had to do. I encouraged them to ask any questions they had that came into their minds. They asked personal questions about my family. They wanted to know my passion and if I walk my talk. They asked how I lead and what I expect of teachers. Our meeting lasted three hours.

In the weeks that followed the meeting, I had many one-on-one conversations with teachers who were interested in Deerfield. They seemed to want to know if this guy was for real. Teachers also expressed their anxiety and fear of the unknown in the opening of a new school. They wanted to know what kind of support they would have and reassurance that they would be successful. I also had a number of teachers who asked me to come and talk to them in their classrooms and to see how they taught. This all helped in my connection with staff to listen, share, and affirm them. It was a great first step in team development.

In late March of 2000, we posted all the staff positions for the school. This made me think back to my final interview for the principal's position for Deerfield and the final question asked by Dr. Rita Traynor, the assistant superintendent. She said, "Richard, you are going to hire a lot of teachers for Deerfield. What do you look for in hiring good teachers?" I told her the most important quality I look for is a passion and love for kids. There was a long pause and silence. I think she expected me to say more. She asked about their experience, education, and other qualifications. I said that I expected them to come with that, but the key for me was that they loved the students. That is a teacher who is selfless with a passion to meet the needs of every student. When I think of selflessness, this anonymous quote comes to mind, "A good teacher is like a candle—it consumes itself to light the way for others." That is the teacher who makes significant connections with his or her students. If they don't know something, they will find it and learn it to help their students.

This has held true over my many years as a principal. I have worked with some teachers with a great résumé and credentials who taught well but never connected with the students. On the other hand, I have worked with teachers with a great love for children and learning who may have not had the university credentials or great grades but had the heart. The heart teachers connected and made a great difference in the lives of students. These are the kind of teachers we all want for our children. This passion, selflessness, and ability to connect is something one senses in a teacher through spending time with them. I have spent hours with candidates for a position talking about them, their experiences, the school, and their feelings about children and education. I want to get to know them. I am hiring a person not a teacher. For me there is something that just clicks. Their love for kids, passion, and selflessness comes through so clearly. I have had great experiences with this through the years. When I have felt a connection with a person, they have proven to be an outstanding teacher. These teachers make a school very special. There is a richness to the culture.

We went through an extensive interviewing process. The assistant superintendent and I asked the same questions to all applicants. It was very interesting that the school board and the teachers' union had agreed to a hands off policy for the first year. I did not have to go by the teacher contract in hiring. For example, many times you have to take the most senior person for a position. I had the freedom to hire by quality of the person and the development of teams. We did not hire everyone who applied. We hired the ones most suitable to the plans and program of the school. I also had the opportunity to hire new staff from outside the district to fill the open positions. Staff was offered a position and had to sign a statement agreeing to the attributes of the school: teaming, multi-age grouping, parents as partners, integration of technology, the house concept, character development, thematic instruction, and our form of discipline as a part of the acceptance of their position. It was a serious pact we developed to insure the success of our program.

As soon as staff was hired in March, we began to have staff meetings. We met every other week and began the process of learning and developing the concepts for our school. I set up the kindergarten through fourth-grade house teams of five teachers. They quickly began the process of bonding and developing their relationship as a team and the concepts for their house. In early April, I brought in a consultant on multi-age grouping to begin our staff orientation. We developed our timeline for activities and training leading up to the opening of our school. Our twice-a-month meetings kept staff updated on the construction of the building and gave us time for working on the development of the program. Staff could not wait to get into the building to get a feel for what is was going to be like. In the midst of construction, we took tours through the dirt and grime, the bricks and mortar, so staff could stand and get a sense of the formation of the houses and room configuration. It added to the excitement of the creation of our school. During the last quarter of the school year, I sent staff (or attended with staff) to a number of conferences that covered specific areas that needed to be addressed in the creation of our program, i.e., multi-age classrooms, full-day kindergarten, Spanish, etc. We also made school visits with staff to programs similar to what we were going to develop. One of the most beneficial was a visit by a large representative of staff to Key School in Indianapolis, Indiana. This was very helpful for staff to see a school (like the one we were opening) functioning and gather information and ideas for our school development. It also helped to have staff talk with teachers who had gone through what they were going through. It gave them assurance that they could do it.

Opening a school is like birthing a child. It is painful and causes high levels of stress and anxiety. Yet at the same time it is filled with exhilaration and is extremely rewarding. We all went through all those emotions in the process of our school's development. I remember the frustration expressed in conversations I had with teachers, the doubts and the fears of "can we do this?" Everyone wanted to do his or her best. Then I also remember the day when one of my staff came up to me in the hall and shared that she had been in teaching for over twenty years, but this was the first time she felt she was really teaching. There were also many times of celebration when a goal was accomplished in those first few hard years.

In late June 2000, the summer before Deerfield opened, the whole staff spent a week together at a nice site near the school. We began the week with a facilitator working on the creation of our school team. One of the facilitators knew me very well, which helped the staff know me better, hearing it from someone who had worked with me for years. The facilitator started our session having staff tell their story and what brought them to Deerfield. This was a wonderful activity. We had staff that had worked together for years that learned things about each other they had never known. At times it was very moving as people shared deeply from their hearts.

We did a personal profile activity called North, South, East, and West. This included a discussion of different personalities and how they work together. It was very helpful in giving our staff a better understanding of each other and that many times the differences we have are due to personalities and not attitude. It was a rich activity that helped us see that we need each other and our different points of view to have the best outcome in our discussions because it allows us to see things from a different perspective.

I have found in building a culture in a school that people want deeper relationships, more transparency and care. They want people to be genuine. Bringing people together in activities like this establishes intimacy and trust. It establishes deep connections throughout the staff. So many times in school and organizations employees function on a very shallow level of relationships. A deeper understanding of each other and sharing from the heart has a tremendous effect on the richness of the culture of the organization. In a school setting, this is transmitted to the students and parents.

After our team building, we then moved into a discussion on the decision making process we would use in our building. During that week we did professional development on multi-age grouping and the delivery of curriculum. Staff worked on the realignment of our curriculum to facilitate instruction. Training was provided on the form of discipline we were going to use in the school. We used the philosophy of Dr. William Glasser; reality therapy and control theory. This is a way of working with children that is centered on responsibility and includes the student in the discipline process, which gave consistency to how we worked with all our students. Our staff worked throughout the summer on curriculum and developing their team relationships. Teachers worked hundreds of unpaid hours with their teams to prepare for the opening of the school. I continued to send letters to our students and parents through the summer to keep them informed and help them feel a part of their new school. We kept them updated on the construction and what we were doing as a staff. Staff also sent letters to their students to start developing their relationship and the feeling of being a part of their new class and house.

The two weeks prior to the opening of the school, staff met at the same location as we had in the spring. They received more training and support in the setting up of a multi-age classroom and instruction in that setting. We did a lot of work on team development, curriculum alignment, and how we were going to start the first few weeks of school. The school was still in construction, so we were unable to get into the building.

I was going into first grade the year Deerfield opened so I was one of the students that had a choice about going. I didn't want to go to a new school, so my mom didn't make me. When it was time for me to be in third grade and my

Richard L. Njus

sister would be starting kindergarten, my mom said she wanted us to go to Deerfield. We entered the lottery and my sister's number was 110. I was hoping that we wouldn't have to go because I didn't want to have to make new friends and learn a new system. But we made it in.

Looking at it now, I'm so glad. I felt like I learned more because I wasn't limited to just third-grade stuff. We were able to work with kids from all the grades and our "house" was like a 130-person family. We had more teachers to work with and had more students to become friends with. When it was time for me to go to fourth grade, I knew my teachers and the other kids, and I didn't worry about it all summer.

I feel very fortunate that I was able to go to Deerfield Elementary.

Taylor, sixth grader

Touching Hearts, Educating Minds   73

Chapter 6

Here We Come, Ready or Not

"We are all faced with a series of great opportunities brilliantly disguised as impossible situations."

Charles Swindoll

We had great opportunities, but when we opened the doors to Deerfield on August 28, 2000, the building was not completed, and we were beginning a program that we had never used. All these thoughts run through your mind: What did we get ourselves into? Can we really do this? Did we bite off more than we can chew? It isn't even finished. And on and on.

On the Friday before the building was to open on Monday, the inspectors gave clearance for us to occupy the building. The whole staff worked day and night throughout the weekend to move in. It was like a long slumber party. I think we had more take out pizza and pop than I have had in my whole life that weekend. On Monday the doors were open, and we welcomed our new students to their new school. I think we were running on pure adrenalin. You could cut the excitement and energy with a knife.

There were still parts of the school that were not completed. The cafeteria floor was bare cement, and we had no tables and chairs. We had to picnic for a couple of weeks before furniture arrived and the floor was finished. Our library was not finished for months. The school was not totally complete until November. The first day of school started with an assembly to introduce everyone and to talk about our school. We introduced all staff, everyone who worked in our building, talked about our responsibility to each other and that we were all working together to learn and grow to our potential. We wanted students to see how we are all connected. We shared our dreams for learning, expectations for character, and goals to be a caring community of learners. Parents were welcome at the assembly. We wanted to make it a family affair. It was a great kick off to our school year. After the assembly, teachers took their students to their respective houses, and the five teachers in each house had activities to start to develop their house identity. My charge to the staff was that they did not have to teach any of the curriculum content the first two weeks but work on building class and house relationships. This is the culture work that needs to be in place in a successful classroom and school.

The first few months, we met weekly in assemblies as a whole school to create the cultural expectations for our school. The first two years we had a fair number of discipline problems. Because we had developed our discipline plan together, we were all consistent with our approach to dealing with problems. All staff worked with students in the same way, using the same techniques in dealing with misbehavior. During our first year, we created a school pledge, which we said together every morning with the pledge of allegiance and announcements. Our pledge was, "Deerfield Explorers are caring, responsible community members who respect themselves, others, and their environment." Over

Richard L. Njus

time, the pledge is all we had to use in correcting students. The Deerfield culture of respect, responsibility, and care had long-lasting effects on our students. This is reflected in the following letter from a parent.

Deerfield not only gave my son, Shaban, a great elementary level education, but it also gave him skills that will help him navigate through life.

There is a poster on the cafeteria wall at school that says, "Character is something you do when no one is watching." When Shaban started in fifth grade (in Novi Meadows—new school), he was having a hard time dealing with a fellow student. The student would "swipe stuff" off of Shaban's desk. Shaban had brought this problem home a few times, but his dad and I wanted him to handle this on his own. One night while his dad and I were giving him some suggestions on how to handle this situation, his younger brother, Kian, said, "You should just swipe all your stuff back." Without hesitation, Shaban's reply was, "But character is something you do when no one is watching."

I had always wondered do the kids realize the importance of our Deerfield pledge? Do they read all the messages on these posters? Do they understand the teachers when they talk about making good choices? Now I know the answer and it is a resounding "yes"; they do, and it is understood and absorbed and used as a moral compass. This is entirely due to climate and "culture" that all the staff have created at Deerfield. We feel very fortunate to have benefitted from their collective wisdom, hard work, and passion.

Fairyal, parent

With the culture of expectation of responsible students in place, peer pressure was an important factor in student behavior. I remember students coming up to me and asking me to talk to a new student who was doing something wrong, and they would say, "We don't do that here."

Another factor in behavior of students is engagement. Dr. Larry Lazotte, an expert in school improvement, said in a meeting with our school district, "The proof of the effectiveness of a school can be determined by the engagement of students." Engagement in learning also has a great effect on discipline. When students are engaged in learning, they do not have time to get in trouble. I always tell parents when we tour the building that I want them to see if our students are engaged. If they are not, then we are not doing our job. Our percentage of discipline problems after the first couple of years dropped through the floor. As principal, I spent very little time, maybe five percent, on discipline.

The first two years were exhausting. Teachers were there day and night, working to stay ahead of our students in the development of our program. I arranged substitute teachers for staff who were developing different levels of curriculum. When we aligned our curriculum vertically rather than horizontally, we had to revise the district and state curriculum. We wanted to have a curriculum that our students could learn through rather then be held back by grade level expectations. This was defined as a continuous progress model. We also developed a two-year cycle for our social studies and science instruction to address the instruction in our two-level multi-age classrooms. Our full-day kindergarten program was developed by our four kindergarten teachers after much research and visiting other programs. Our program is academically and developmentally appropriate. Our kindergarten staff revised the program yearly to reflect what we had discovered in the learning process of our students. For example, in our district, the grade-level expectation in reading was that a child leaving kindergarten would read at an A level. We found that the majority of our students read at a C level or higher. That is where we set the bar. We have found over the years that the effectiveness of our program has raised the level of our expectation for all students. Staff continually revised and enriched our program. Grade-level teams met on a regular basis to discuss and develop our program. They revised curriculum as needed to meet the needs of our students. We continually shared with parents how we were progressing.

In the fall of 2001, Dr. Parker Palmer, author of *The Courage to Teach*, visited Deerfield for a day. He spent the morning walking the building, talking with staff, students, and parents. In the afternoon, I hired substitute teachers for all my staff, and Dr. Palmer met with us and discussed our school. I had asked him prior to his visit to judge whether our school was modeling what a school should be doing in the best practice of teaching and learning. He affirmed this and said he was very impressed with our school. Something he said that haunts me now was, "You are like a satellite, you are flying out here, and the forces of tradition, your district , the state and federal government, and your own comfort zone will try to pull you back into traditionalism." Sadly, over the years we have found this prophecy to be true. Changes in curriculum have forced us to change our program. Testing expectations by our state and the national expectations have tried to pull our satellite in. The pressure from the district to have all schools the same was a pressure that we dealt with every year. But all the pressures to pull back to traditionalism failed.

Every year we have had many visits from professors from universities and other educators. We would always ask them for their assessment of our school and program. The assessments have always been very complimentary. I received frequent requests from schools to have their teachers come and spend a day with our staff to observe how our program functions. Deerfield became a learning center for other schools. Our teachers mentored many teachers from around the state and our own district in our instructional practices. We were honored by visits from educators from around the world. I have toured the building with a delegation of seventy-five educators from Korea, a group of more than forty Japanese educators, and had numerous tours with Chinese educators. Touring with Chinese educators culminated in a chance for me to visit China, where I was asked to speak at two conferences on how we deal with high risk testing and on the building of the affective aspect of a school culture. After I returned from China, I worked with the U.S./China Center at Michigan State University and the Sunwah Education Foundation from China in the planning and development of a pre-K/kindergarten school to be built in Beijing, China. Today there is a school in Beijing, China, with many of the attributes of Deerfield. I visit their Web site frequently to see how they are progressing. It is heartwarming when one realizes one's school has touched people on the other side of the world.

Richard L. Njus

The development and revision of our program was an ongoing process. We continually looked at how our teaching is a reflection of best practices. Staff worked together well in creating a program that reflected the desires of the cadre's mission. We truly became a school that met the learning styles, interests, and learning stages of all students. The first few years I had many conversations with parents about the programs and the differences from a traditional school. Areas that needed clarification were: the delivery of curriculum in a multi-age setting, our no-homework policy, full-day kindergarten, and the house setting. We continually used research on learning to help parents understand the philosophy of the school. I wrote newsletters and had meetings to inform and bring our parents along with us on our journey of learning. The first year, I answered a lot of questions. The second year, there were fewer questions. And the third year, the parents answered the questions for each other. This was an outgrowth in our cultural development of transparent trust by our parents. Because we were transparent, truthful, and had gained their trust, they no longer questioned what we were doing or our motives. We had established an intimacy in our connections with parents.

During our first few years, we as a staff did a lot of work on teaming. We had an outside facilitator come in and work with us, we did personality profiles and book studies. I think that the most effective work we did was facilitated by our own staff. These sessions were very helpful in getting us through the first few years of toil and struggle. It was the work we needed to do to help us connect with each other, which in turn enriched our connection with students.

Teachers are role models. We teach more by what we do than by what we say. Students are very perceptive and know if we are just using words or if we live what we say.

At the end of three years, staff felt like they could stop and take a breath. The program was set and the culture of the school was becoming very evident. But as Dr. Parker Palmer prophesied, the forces of our school district, the state and federal government, and the community were trying to pull us back into the sphere of traditionalism. For example, the adoption of a district math program forced us to go from multi-age instruction of math by grade level. This change happened even after I personally asked the committee and the representatives from the textbook company if we could teach the program in a multiage setting. Since then I don't know how many times staff has said that our first two years we taught the best math that they have ever taught. The writing program has had the same results.

We have also had to fight to keep full-day kindergarten in our building each year. It is the integral foundation for our program. Jealousy and misperceptions of our program in the community and other schools continually applied pressure for us to change to be like everyone else. We also had to revisit the support of the school board for siblings attending their brother or sister's school. It was established in the beginning of the development of the school that families would have priority and siblings would have first right to spaces as they opened. Our parents were very active in supporting our efforts to maintain the purity of our program. We continually had parents requesting their children transfer to Deerfield. I held monthly tours to accommodate the requests for tours of our school.

In our fifth year, we revised and enriched our writing, phonics, and spelling curriculum. By our standards, this is an area in which we were low in our state assessment. In the revision of our curriculum, we found that we had to move our whole curriculum down half-a-grade level because our students were performing well-above grade level. On our state assessments, we have performed very high. In our 2005/06 school year we received 100% in both reading and math. One cannot do better than that. And in response to all the work staff did in writing in 2006, our writing assessment scores rose significantly. That is outstanding.

The proof of our success with our community is that we had to have a lottery every year to fill open seats because the demand was so high. We would average eighty or more students on our waiting list for kindergarten and twenty to thirty students on our list for first through fourth grades. Every year we would have parents from outside our school district sign a lease agreement on an apartment to establish residency to get in the lottery. If they would get into our school, they would move into the district. If they did not, they would break their lease. We also pulled many students from private school.

As immigrants from an Asian country where academics is priority, when we had our kids, we thought that they would have the best of both worlds. Born into a country which had the latest and greatest advances in most fields, be it science or arts or sports with parents who could teach the values of education and hard work.

In the five and half years my son has been schooling, Deerfield is his fourth school. We started off with the Montessori; pros: great in academics and rigid in character development; cons: socially inhibiting. There was zero parent involvement.

The next attempt was parochial school system: again great for theoretical moral values; cons: academics did not flex to the child's academic needs.

The first attempt at public school came about a year before we moved to Deerfield. The toughest year of our lives when we saw both our kids taking several steps back academically and they had more "fun" activities than we cared to count. When I brought it to the attention of the educating authorities at the school, I was shown the Michigan education Web site and asked to download information so I may teach my kids on my own at home.

So here I had kids going to school for almost eight hours, and the few hours they spent at home, I had to continue to tutor them. It was a very frustrating period when I finally gave in and decided to apply through the Deerfield "lottery" system—a concept I never did agree with. With all of us paying the same taxes, why would only a few selected randomly get a "special" education? Sheer desperation drove me to do it.

Today both my kids are at Deerfield and I cannot emphasize how well balanced the school is. Both my kids' grade three and grade one learn something new every day with advancement academically as well as socially. Finally, I do not hear the phrase "school is boring" anymore. I have stopped the Kumon math classes as they are barely able to keep up with educational activities happening in the school. They have a good deal of fun, a very diverse group of people and cultures they meet and learn to accept.

Deerfield has been a very nice educational experience and as working parents I think this has been our best option for education in the great country we have adopted. It is a school that does not underestimate a child's capacity to learn, assimilate and express. I surely believe it lays a good foundation for the kids of those families who want the best in both character and education for the kids.

Nisha Chellam, parent

Richard … I visited Deerfield yesterday with the GVSU (Grand Valley State University) student teachers and their field coordinator. I have spent most of my thirty-five year teaching career frustrated with the limitations public education seemed to put on student learning. During my career, I worked for change but never had much success outside of my own classroom or teaching team. I left Deerfield so refreshed knowing that there was an institution doing it the right way! Keep up the great work instilling "The Joy of Learning"!

Carolyn Schmidt,
Grand Valley State University

Chapter 7

Parents as Partners

"Parents are a child's first and most important teacher."

A critical component of Deerfield's success and the success of any quality school are the parents. It was key in our development that we create a vital partnership between home and school. The circle of our school community embraced the parent as the child's first and most important teacher. This partnership with parents is called "social capital" in Robert D. Putnam and Lewis M. Feldstein's book *Better Together*. It is the social network, reciprocity, mutual assistance, and trust that a healthy organization needs. It is a caring, open relationship, a strong connection between parents and teachers. We created a school where parents felt welcome. The first thing that people see when they walk in our school is a welcome sign. Parents have volunteer opportunities and learning opportunities. Our school design incorporated a room for their use. Former Secretary of Education Richard Riley said, "The American family is the rock on which a solid education can and must be built." We honored this and affirmed our families. We defined a family as the group of people you live with.

Over the years we developed a very strong parent partnership. They provided tremendous support for our programs, volunteering and fund raising that was outstanding. Our parents became true partners in learning. Former New Jersey Senator (and retired NBA basketball player) Bill Bradley once said, "Trying to educate children without the involvement of their family is like trying to play a basketball game without all the players on the court." At Deerfield we wanted all the players on the court. We continually encouraged our parents' involvement and kept them informed of their great influence on learning. Parent involvement is crucial to our school success. It all comes down to keeping the children at the center in all we do. This brings to mind one of my favorite quotes, "None of us stands so tall as when we stoop to help a child." Helping children is what teaching, parenting, and volunteering is all about … a shared venture, a cooperative understanding, a labor of love. The staff of Deerfield and our parents shared the venture; they lived the labor of love in our students' journey in learning.

A child's learning begins well before he or she attends school. The greatest milestones in learning occur not in the classroom, but in the home. The period from zero to five years of age is very important in brain development. Children learn 50 percent of their vocabulary before turning five years old. A child's prior knowledge and experiences have a great effect on their learning. That is what parents give them in the home. We affirmed parents as their child's primary teacher.

There is an overwhelming amount of research on parents and their influence on a child's learning, not only before children get to school, but also while they attend school. Parents set the tone for learning, and teachers nourish it and help it grow. Parents' influence on a child's learning is a strong determiner in their success. We as educators know that. Sam Sava, the former President of National Association of Elementary Middle School Principals, said, "Children absorb, by emotional and intellectual osmosis, as many unspoken lessons about love and work in their home as they do the spoken lessons of the classroom. It's not just speech and early literacy that good mothers and fathers confer, but flesh-and-blood examples of how to live."

Research has shown that students attending schools that maintain frequent contact with their communities outperform those in other schools. Children whose parents are in touch with the school score higher on standardized tests than children of similar aptitude and family background whose parents are not involved. Students who are failing in school improve dramatically when their parents are called in to help. This reminds me of an experience I had as a second grade teacher. One of my students (I'll call him John) was having serious difficulty in school. I called his home and set up a meeting with his mother. She came in very nervous and reserved as if she had a chip on her shoulder. I tried to make her feel comfortable. In our discussion I sensed that her experience in school had not been a positive one. I shared that John was having difficulty in reading, math, and by his actions communicated he did not like school. I shared the plan for what I was doing in class to help John. I asked her what she felt about it and if she had any recommendations or insights that might help me with John. I encouraged his mother to read with him and listen to him read at home.

In the flow of our conversation, I brought up a need I had

for parents to help in class. I asked if she would like to come in and volunteer. She was very apprehensive. I told her she would only have to listen to kids read and that it would be a big help to me. I said that mostly her volunteering would encourage her son. Seeing her in his school would send a very important message to John about how she felt about his learning. She said she would try it. I told her she would do a great job, and I would be there to help if she needed it. She came in the first day with fear in her eyes, but over time she began to enjoy her time and came in with a smile and shared a lot of excitement for working with the children. After a few months, what was really exciting is that John began to change dramatically. He had a joy for learning, and he began having success in reading and math. Through the year John experienced very positive growth. Most of all he loved learning and felt good about himself. It was interesting that toward the end of school, John's mother stopped me in the hall. I thought she wanted to talk to me about John. No, she wanted to tell me she wanted John's brother in my class the next fall, and she wanted to know when she could come in and volunteer. I don't think John would have experienced the success he did if his mother hadn't partnered with me by coming in and helping in the classroom.

Knowing the importance of parent involvement in their child's learning, it is a shame our society is not helping parents to honor and support the family. Although everyone talks about the importance of raising children, the cultural climate has become subtly less hospitable to parents who put children first. This is not because parents love their children less, but because a "job culture" is expected at the expense of a "family culture."

We realized what we were up against in our culture and appreciated what our parents did for our students at Deerfield. Schools cannot be hermetically sealed and succeed without the help of parents. Deerfield's parents' influence on our learners had a far-reaching effect on them. With our school parent council, we developed many opportunities for parents to be involved. Their volunteering was exceptional, with many parents involved in classrooms and for special events. Just having a parent stop in for lunch with their kids makes a great difference. An adult talking with children about school activities outside their school setting gives a child's learning importance. Staff and I encouraged our parents and community to be an integral part of our students through encouragement and supporting their learning. We had a high percentage of dual career families and made a point to tell our parents how much we appreciated them and the tremendous impact they had on the learning of our students.

As a part of our program, we had parents and students share in parent-teacher conferences. We developed student-led conferences. Over the years our conferencing evolved and changed in form. They were highly effective. Parents were very complimentary of conferences where their child was involved. It was really a sight to see students talking to their parents about their successes and challenges. It helps parents to grasp their child's learning style, and parents were also very impressed that their children could articulate effectively about their own learning, their strengths and weaknesses. Both parents and students communicated the positive effect of our conferences.

Deerfield was proactive in creating an open door policy from day one for parents. I encouraged parents to be the advocates for their children. We wanted an environment where parents felt free to ask questions. We encouraged open dialogue between parents, teachers, and the principal. I told parents many times that they did not have to make an excuse or feel apprehensive to come and talk to me about anything. There were no dumb questions. Our open atmosphere for conversation did much to enrich our learning community. I found over the years that there was a very relaxed atmosphere between parents and staff. There was a freedom to be open.

When parents are partners with us in learning, we as staff have to support them in their quest to be the best they can. Parenting is not an easy task or one that can be taken lightly. In our world, today's parents must figure out how to protect their children from what comes in conflict with their values and what is harmful to their well-being. Sometimes, parents have to be counterculture. They counter the culture with their core beliefs and values. The school needs to support parents in helping their children connect with a meaningful world outside of the family. We found this especially important with the diversity of our population and the cultures and religious beliefs our families represented. Parents are their children's most important role models. I am reminded of this every day. Under the plastic protector on my desk, I have a card from one of my sons that says, "Dad, I hope I can be like you someday." It makes me proud, but it is also sobering, sending a message each time I look at it. It makes me sit a little taller and think about my actions. All parents are faced with this challenge. Their school needs to be there to support them.

We provided a number of activities over the years to support our parents. I did a book study with parents on *The Shelter of Each Other* by Dr. Mary Pipher. This book has a great focus on the challenges for parents living in our society. It goes through a number of scenarios of families. We had great discussion. It was a rich experience from which we all grew. Our staff conducted sessions for parents on reading, math, writing, and literacy. These were very helpful in providing parents with information that would help them support at home what their children were experiencing in school.

I also did a session on discipline, using our school's approach to working with our students. The program was founded on responsibility. It involved students in the discipline process and helped them to take responsibility for their actions. We talked a lot about choices. One thing we would tell students was: you are a sum total of your choices. We talked about the decisions we make as parents and educators when working with children. How do we balance freedom and discipline when dealing with students? We want our children to be responsible, respectful, and successful, but it can't be forced or coerced. Are we tough or gentle? What is the key component that makes the difference? It is the power of love. We have a giant poster on our office wall that says, "Where love is deep, much will be accomplished." Many parents commented on how helpful the sessions were for them at home.

I produced two newsletters each month to provide information and to encourage parents in their quest to be the best for their kids. We wanted parents to know that we know that there is not an easy guidebook to parenting. It is hard work, and we all make a lot of mistakes along the way. It is a learning experience. It is setting high standards for our kids and demanding that they are met and not accepting excuses when that doesn't happen. It is passing on our family values even though they may be counterculture. It is not easy, but the payoff is fantastic. I've lost count of the number of times parents have commented on how our school community has helped them be better, more effective parents.

Mother Teresa said, "We must bring our children back to the center of our care and concern. This is the only way that our world can survive because our children are the only hope for the future." I continually thanked our parents for keeping their kids at the center and for all their support. I often say it takes all of us working together to do the best for our students.

Within our school, we had a rich diversity of students from around the world. I often said that, as I stood at the door each morning, I welcomed my little united nations into our building. It was remarkable the number of countries represented by our students. Our community needed to open our arms and embrace all cultures. We set up a parent committee to help us all better understand our cultures. It was wonderful to listen to the discussions and see the connections in the diverse group begin to form. In order to celebrate our diversity and to sensitize us to a better understanding of our cultures, this committee developed our international festival. The festival was created by and for our parents and students. Parents would set up booths with artifacts from their country, items to help others gain a better understanding of their country, culture, and food. Parents and children would dress in the clothing from their country. We would have special performances of music, dance, and other forms of entertainment from their countries. It was a heart-warming time. I loved seeing our students dressed up. They were so proud. It was also so rich to observe the interaction of parents as they shared together in our celebration. It was a phenomenal experience for students, parents, and staff. Parents were great role models of understanding of diversity for their children. It was great to see countries represented in the same room who had been in conflict or at war with each other for years, yet in our learning community, there was a rich sense of desire to understand and get along, to celebrate our differences rather than judge them.

This carried over into the classroom as parents and students shared from their cultural background. We even named our cafeteria the International Café, placing flags from around the world around the whole room. We first took a survey of our parents and their country of origin and started with those flags. We later added flags when it was drawn to our attention that someone's flag was missing. The international environment of the school adds a rich ingredient to the education of our students in preparing them to take their places in our international society. We see this as an integral part of educating the whole child.

When I think back over the past six years, I am most moved by the stories of students who had had negative experiences in their past school, or had been failing as a learner, and at Deerfield caught the joy of learning. Many parents shared with me the stories of their children whose lives changed by attending Deerfield. Our deep partnership with our parents made a tremendous difference. I remember one mother telling me she had to drag her son into school at his last school and now he doesn't even want to go on vacation, he loves school so much.

In October of our seventh year, I had a mother whose son had recently transferred to our school stop in my office. She said that in his last school her son had been labeled as a troublemaker and hated school. He would not read or write. The reason she wanted to come into my office was to share the joy of his progress. He loved school. He was reading and writing. I had not seen him in my office for one discipline issue. His mother said she got her son back. This story was replicated over and over again, as you will read throughout this book. I have had students and parents return here after their children have been out of our school for a few years to share what a difference their learning experience at Deerfield made in their child's success in later grades. I saw this same strong feeling for our school in the tears of staff and students when we left for the summer.

We discussed often why and what made the difference. We are just a school doing what schools do. It reminds me of a quote by Booker T. Washington, "Excellence is to do a common thing in an uncommon way." We were doing what schools do but in an uncommon way. It was the depth and richness of the connection of students, staff, and parents in the joy of learning. The relationship of transparent trust with parents, embracing them as partners in their children's learning added much to the richness of our culture.

Yes, the use of best practices made the difference in our instruction. Our students were performing beyond expectations. The multi-age and the house configuration for learning made a significant difference in learning for the whole child. In the configuration, the major effect on our students was that they knew five teachers for five years. It also created a flow to a student's learning. There was very little transition time from year to year. And the teachers' connections with students were extremely important. Deerfield became a place where students, parents, and staff came together and created something very special that we defined as a caring community of learners. As one staff member said, "We have created one big family here." We shared a rich culture which embraced students, staff, and parents. One of our parents, Elizabeth Copeland, was so touched by our culture that she created the following drawing to depict our school's partnership with parents.

"It takes all of us working together to provide the best for our students"

Richard Njus, Principal Deerfield Elementary

Chapter 8

Culture of Care and Learning

"Being here at this school feels like I am at home. You make me feel special in my heart and in the outside."

Cassidy, third grader

With all the development that went into our school in our program, curriculum, and the beauty of our facility, the definitive reason for parents wanting to come to Deerfield came down to culture. That is what I was told over and over by our families. I have been asked many times how I would define culture. The Merriam-Webster's Desk Dictionary defines culture as: "tillage, cultivation, the act of developing by education and training, refinement of intellectual and artistic taste, the customary beliefs, social forms, and material traits of a racial, religious, or social group."

Customary beliefs, social forms, and material traits resonate with me. Culture to me is that living core that runs through the texture of an organization. It is the heartbeat of the organization. It is core beliefs that permeate an organization. In a school, it is the care and love that surround the learner, the sense of energy for learning, and the understanding for the learner. It is what makes a child who has been turned off by school ignite the flame of learning again. This can be illustrated through an e-mail I received from a parent whom I talk to frequently about life, education, and shared recommendations for books I have found rewarding. She sent me the e-mail after looking in a local bookstore for one of the books I recommended. I was interested in a comment on education in her e-mail.

> I bought the book you recommended but had this thought as I looked at all the titles on education and children…interesting, Richard never gave a recommendation to anything here. And instantly I knew why, because there is a limited narrowness to just "teaching" our children. The extension and outreach of love to their souls is more important.

There is a limited narrowness to just teaching; what a powerful sentence! In the fall 2005, issue of *The Curves Magazine*, Dr. Kent Nerburn said, "We all live in fear of being judged by others, while the empty space between us is waiting to be filled by a simple gesture of honest caring." I have seen that waiting reflected in the eyes of children and adults. It breaks my heart when a teacher does not fill that space with care. A rich culture embodies care and the sensitivity of staff to surround each child with the love and nurturing they need to fill that waiting space. It is that teacher who has the innate ability to connect with his or her students. Parents frequently shared their feelings on our rich culture, which surrounded their children with love and filled that waiting space.

Over the past thirty-five years, I have observed too often the limited narrowness. Teachers who have the book knowledge and follow all the grade level expectations. Teachers who have become master teachers of curriculum, but not of children. Though a child may acquire knowledge, he or she may not experience the fullness of learning. These teachers have missed the mark. "The extension and outreach of love to their souls is more important," my friend said. That is what a rich school culture has—soul. Soul is not something we learn in college, like teaching techniques and curriculum; it is who we are. Culture is the atmosphere created to instill an affect for the students, which helps them to feel loved, supported, and free to take risks, fail, learn, and grow. It is a place where the joy of learning permeates the school.

This was brought to mind by something one of my teachers shared with me about a conversation she had with teacher who had moved from our school who said, "You know we had a great feeling at our school, and Richard used to talk all the time about culture; I never fully understood what he meant. Now that I am in another building I know. We have no culture. There is not that feeling we had at Deerfield." I have said for years that the proof of the richness of culture in a building is noted when someone who has never been in the school comes in, talks to no one, and says, "I feel something special in this place." That is culture. It is a school where children don't want to go on vacation because they are so engaged in the joy of learning. It is a place where children who have felt failure and estrangement feel accepted and energized to learn. It is a place where students feel a connection and affirmation with and from their teachers. I don't know how many times I have talked to parents who say before coming to Deerfield their child didn't want to come to school, but since being in our school their attitude has changed 180 degrees. What is the difference? It is culture.

I have led many tours over the last seven years for school board members, teachers, parents, and administrators looking at our building design in preparation to build a new school. After one of the building tours with a team from another school district and the architect who designed Deerfield, a board member from the team stopped in my office to speak with me. She said, "Our team has visited four schools today. When we walked into your school, I felt something interestingly different from the other schools. This place is special. I have never seen students so engaged in learning. It is great to see best practices in teaching and learning in action. Your school culture is wonderful." We had numerous conversations in the following months about creating a school with a culture that truly touched lives. Her energy and excitement for our school was encouraging and motivational for our whole staff.

When we were honored with a visit from the director of a foundation in China who was working with the U.S./China Center at Michigan State University, we spent hours in discussion about the school. He went around the school filming classrooms and the building structure. He was very impressed with the building, but more impressed with the program and culture of the school. This culminated in my involvement in the design of the building and program for a school that was opened in Beijing, China, in 2005. A key area he wanted me to be involved in was the development of the creativity and affective domain of the program. The other area was my input on the design of the interior of the school to create a flow for learning. In our planning for the school, they brought together professors from various universities and from the U.S./China Center at Michigan State University, educators from Sesame Street, LeapFrog, the Hands on Museum in San Francisco, and the George Lucas Foundation. We wanted to take the best from the Chinese and U.S. educational system in creating a program to meet all students' needs for an excellent education. My role was to keep the principal's perspective on the planning. I was charged to keep the reality factor of the program functionality in the school. This was a great personal experience. Once again it was an affirmation that what we were doing at Deerfield was right.

I have had the privilege of opening two schools. As I have said, it is energizing and exhausting. In my experience, it takes three years to create the culture of a school. It is a fascinating experience to watch a culture evolve. It is also hard work. It is very important that staff is trained and participate fully in the development of the culture. It is heart work. It is generated through a staff with a sense of vocation. A key factor in the culture of a school is the leader. The principal's purpose, personality, and passion play an integral part in the development of the culture of the school. That person sets the tone for the building

Culture comes from the heart and not the head. One of my favorite quotes is, "Where the passion of your heart meets the needs of the world, this is your joy," by Fredrick Bueckner. This has a lot to do with where culture comes from. Culture is generated from passion. It is what one feels. That is a heart thing. When I think of all the schools that are put forth by the media or government as successful, it is always led by a passionate leader. When they talk about their school, they show their heart and their passion. They may have a great program, but what drives the program is the passion generated through the culture of the school. This is extended through the teachers and staff to the students. The success comes through the extension and outreach of love to the souls of the students. It is honoring all the individuals in the school—students, parents, and staff. All staff are role models of this. Teachers are the key, and their ability to connect with students is imperative to creating an engaging culture for learning. Parker Palmer in his book *The Courage to Teach* emphasizes this in the following quotes:

> What we teach will never take unless it connects with the inward, living core of our students' lives, with our students' inward teacher...Good teachers possess a capacity for connectedness. The connections made by teachers are held not in their methods but in their hearts. Small wonder, then, that teaching tugs as the heart, opens the heart, even breaks the heart, and the more one loves teaching, the more heart breaking it can be.

That depth of teaching is also very enriching and fulfilling. To emphasize this further I share a quote from Mary Pipher from her book *The Shelter of Each Other,*

> Children need to believe that the world is an interesting and safe place. The relationship between children

and their teachers isn't incidental, but is the central component of their learning. Human development occurs within the context of real relationships. We learn from whom we love.

The teacher in the classroom and his or her connections with students determines the depth of the culture. I can't think of a better way to illustrate this effect of teacher connections than through a letter written to a teacher moving out of state. I love the way Noah talks about his connections with his teacher.

> Julie,
> OMG, as Emma's friends would say, I can't believe the impact you've had on my child this year!!! I'm writing to tell you that we are really having to process your departure with Noah. I thought that leaving Sherry last year would be hard but it is nothing compared to how Noah is expressing his feelings about leaving you. Now, I "know" my kid and transition is hard for him period but you clearly have made an impact in one "short" school year. I hope you take this e-mail as an additional testament to the "hero" you've been. It's not meant to make you feel bad because I know that one year with you will last a lifetime for Noah.
>
> He told me Mrs. Kaufman is leaving and I hurt inside and I told him . . . you changed from Mrs. G's room, you can do this too to Mr. McCurdy's room, and he said, "But no one is like ME as much as Mrs. Kaufman." So I asked him how that was possible and

he said, "No one sees inside me like Mrs. Kaufman and no one knows how heavy worry is to carry around." I asked him if his other teachers couldn't help carry the worry and he said, "Maybe, but no one makes my heart feel better like she does because she's felt it before."

I hope you know how much you've meant to Noah (us) this year as we've traveled the road of his first big change. I know he'll be fine with Ron next year. He'll miss your touch nonetheless!!!!!!!!!!!!

I can't say it enough in the coming weeks but THANK YOU for taking him into your heart and understanding.

Claudia

Noah defined well the connection of a student with a teacher. It is a teacher who "sees inside and knows how heavy the worry is to carry around." It is the inner connection of the soul of a teacher to the soul of a child. What a difference it makes.

I think a lot about what makes the radical change in a teacher to make them want to connect with students. As we know, not all teachers do. To some, teaching is the place they can teach a subject area they like or is just a good job with summers off. But what makes certain teachers and sometimes grabs a hold of those not so passionate teachers to give them the desire to connect with all kids? I would like to share a poem that I read at a retreat, which I think will help us get at what makes the difference.

Poem (untitled, about Discovery)
By Lisa Wiens Heinsohn

I have been selling peanuts at a little tourist stand
my whole life with my back to the Grand Canyon, and
until yesterday
never once have I turned around
Yesterday someone passed me with a mirror and I split wide
open.
Trembling, trembling with my eyes shut, almost afraid to see,
I turned,
dared to look,
and before me was the ecstasy of light,
of red rock,
of immensity beyond imagination
right in my backyard.
Ahhhhhh, my heart cries, it sputters, it groans
All the years! All the years selling peanuts! What have I done,
dear
God, where have I been?
Abandoned, I have not waited
even to tie my shoes. My peanuts lie, torn paper bags, strewn
on the
ground,
the cash register open, dollar bills flapping in the wind. All
forgotten,
relics.
I stumble around, around the vastness of this unimaginable
beauty,
My heart breaking at each new crevice, each
Canyon wall of light and dust and rock and pinon pine,
Each sunrise,
Sunset,
The possibilities only beginning,
A galaxy of rock and splendor to explore.

Let my bones lie in some corner of this miracle, this mystery.
I will die happy.

What is the switch that is tripped that releases the flood of emotion, love for kids, and the desire to help all students be their best? For the peanut vendor, he saw the Grand Canyon and its splendor, and everything was changed forever. His life had new meaning. He left all behind to pursue it. What makes the difference for educators? It is when we turn from facing the chalk or white board and see our students anew. When we look into their eyes and see their vast talent and desire to learn. One connects one's soul with his students' souls when one grasps the depth of the richness of their minds and hearts. One feels a passion and drive to help students be all they can be, realize their great potential, and be fulfilled in the reality of who they are. Teachers, like the peanut vendor, who look into the grand canyon of their students' eyes will never be the same.

This is why hiring quality teachers for our schools is so critically important. We want teachers of passion and soul who connect with their students. One example of the impact of the connectedness of teachers and the culture of a school on students is reflected in a conversation I had with a teacher from another building. She came up to me at a professional development day for our whole school district in another elementary. She said she wanted to share an experience she'd had in the high school the past week. She was talking to one of the high school students, and in the conversation she asked the student where she attended elementary. The student replied, "I went to Deerfield for the fourth grade, and it was the best year of my life." That was the first year, and we were just starting the program and development of culture. To know we touched a student so deeply the first year says volumes about the depth of the Deerfield culture.

Following is another example from an eighth-grade student, which captures how the connection with one teacher changed his life in his own words.

> *It feels like forever ago that I first went to Deerfield. I went to another Novi elementary school for kindergarten, where I spent the majority of the year suspended and moving from classroom to classroom. My parents decided to send me to the new school in Novi, and I become part of the first group of students to attend Deerfield.*
>
> *The year began with some of the same issues, then Mr. Njus decided to move me into Mrs. Kaufman's class. I was a first grader being moved into a third and fourth-grade classroom. Before that, I had gone to multiple classes, none of which seemed to work for me. In Mrs. Kaufman's class, I was different than anyone else, but the class was different than those I had experienced. Instead of having to go everywhere and being forced around, I was able to move at my own pace, as long as I was learning. I would sometimes do my schoolwork inside a cabinet in the coat room of the adjacent classroom, which was empty. In "Miss Invisible's" room, as we called it, I did my work in nice, peaceful tranquility. I even made a "welcome mat" and used Mrs. Kaufman's lamp to light up my work. Looking back, that was rather odd, but it helped me as I was adjusting to my new environment.*
>
> *Instead of demanding that I sit down, shut up, and*

do my work, she allowed me to complete my work in my own way. As I would learn, there would be plenty of time for "shut up and do my work" at Meadows [Novi's fifth and sixth-grade building], but that's a story for another day. Sometimes I would go out of the classroom to work on the computer, and Mrs. Kaufman was okay with that too, as long as she knew where I was. I just had to complete my schoolwork and go to specials. In time, as I became more comfortable, I began to spend more time with my classmates. I found that I "fit in."

I'm glad that Mrs. Kaufman had the patience and flexibility that she did, because a lot of teachers don't. It took a while for us to be able to work together effectively. In retrospect, I learned a lot both in her curriculum and outside the curriculum. We both accomplished much after I was given time to adjust to my new surroundings. I remember that Mrs. Kaufman compiled for me a folder of learning choices. I could go through it and decide what to accomplish that day. It must have been a huge effort for her, but at that point, for me it was likely the only way to accomplish anything. She also took the time to listen to me when I was having difficulty, when most other teachers would have already made up their minds on how to handle things. She took the time and she understood me. My behavior wasn't perfect, and I got in trouble. But when I look back, I can at least know that I was always treated fairly and with respect.

Jacob, eighth-grade student

One now begs the question, how do we create this culture? How do we teach leaders to be culture developers? Is this something that can be taught? I don't fully know the answer. I strongly feel that some people are born with the gift of teaching or leading. When I interview teachers for a position, I get the sense that this is their calling and a gift. These teachers have a richness that book learning cannot bring to the classroom. They connect with their students to the soul of their learning. The whole child is enriched by the time they spend in their classroom. I have many times asked people why they are doing what they are doing today. Why did they choose the vocation they chose? Almost every person goes back to a person who touched them in a special way. Many say a teacher. It was not what they taught; it was how they taught it. It was the passion they showed through their teaching.

The rich culture generated in a school is the passion of a staff lived out. So I think the answer to the question of how do we build culture in a school is we have to do heart/soul work. We have to bring educators back to their vocation of love. This cannot be faked. Frank McCourt in his book *Teacher Man* said, "Teaching is like writing, you have to find your tone. And you have to tell the truth. If you put on a mask, they'll find you out every time." We have all the best practices in research of how to teach effectively. When we combine that with the heart of passion generated in a rich school culture, the whole student is enriched.

Dr. Parker Palmer, the author of *The Courage to Teach*, has established centers for teacher renewal in universities and centers around the United States. In these centers teachers and administrators do soul work. They meet on a regular basis over a two-year period with a group searching their hearts and many times reconnecting with the heart of their vocation. There are outstanding stories of renewal from these experiences in Dr. Palmer's book *The Courage to Teach* and Sam M. Intrator's book *Stories of the Courage to Teach, Honoring the Teachers Heart.*

In Deerfield we lived out this concept of teaching where teachers connected with their students. We tried to live our mission, the joy of learning. This came through much open and honest dialogue with staff. We worked to keep our students and their needs at the center of everything we did. It was a growing process. It was at times frustrating and painful when we had to push our selfish issues aside for our students. But in the end it was very rewarding. Mihaly Csikszentmihalyi from the University of Chicago said, "As we strive to educate children, we need to consider the passion they start out with. Once in formal education they tend to lose that spontaneous passion and joy for learning, the greatest challenge for teachers is to encourage young people to find pleasure in the right things." We worked very hard not to cover over our students with our expectations and rules and stifle their joy and excitement for learning. From the time students entered the building in the morning until they left to go home, staff connected with them. I was in the halls in the morning with support staff to greet our students and outside in front of the school in the evening to say goodbye. Daily I walked through the classrooms, watching, talking, and touching students to let them know I cared about them and their learning. It also lets staff know that their principal supports and encourages them.

Staff had many forms of morning meetings to develop a close relationship with their students. The make up of our classrooms with the multi-age house setting helped to draw students together. We stressed character development and promoted caring, respect, and responsibility for each other. We had buddy systems with students in the houses. Older and younger students worked together for many activities. The care modeled by staff was modeled in our students toward each other. It was heartwarming to watch students come in, in the morning, hand in hand. We surrounded our students with love and care, which created a strong family feeling in the school. The passion for education and working with children was sensed throughout the school. Stephen Shapiro said, "When you are living a life of passion, you're almost always making a contribution." What a contribution our staff has made to the health of our school culture through their passion!

Culture is the living core that runs through an organization. At Deerfield we lived that living core of care and energy and joy of learning. It was difficult to explain but was as real as the air we breathe. It had texture and depth. It motivated, encouraged, and supported risk taking. I know its effect; I felt it in the energy of our daily lives as I walked through the school. And I heard it from the students who came back frequently to reconnect with the source of their joy. I remember one student who had many challenges and who challenged and stretched us. On a visit back after being out of the school for a few years, he said, "It even smells good here." Then he came and greeted us all with a hug. Oliver Window Holmes said, "Man's mind stretched to a new idea never returns to its original dimensions." That is what a truly enriching school culture does; it stretches the mind and heart, and it will never be the same again. We learn more and we feel more. I know through my experience at Deerfield that I will never be the same again.

Let me tell you about my school Deerfield Elementary...

Whether you're young or old, Deerfield makes you feel special. Everyone is kind and even the building itself feels friendly. All the teachers are very unique and the principal is no ordinary principal. They never make you feel unwanted. Instead, they make you feel important.

The best thing is you'll be happy practically all the time. As you walk down the hallways of Deerfield, you can feel the "happy air." You can hear laughter, and there is always learning going on. You can be yourself and never be afraid to share your ideas because everyone respects you.

When I come back from summer break and I'm ready to start a new grade, it feels just like coming home after a long vacation. Everything is familiar and I am always welcome. I am so glad I got a chance to come to Deerfield. I think that when I grow up, my best memories of going to school will be these years at Deerfield. Thank you, Mr. Njus, for making the school!

Aria, third grade

Richard L. Njus

Chapter 9

Leadership

"Leaders are people who leave their
footprints in their areas of passion."

Jonathan Byrnes

This brings us to a discussion of leadership style and culture creation. Leadership and culture are intertwined in the fabric of a school. Leadership is not a position we hold; it is defined by those who follow. Peter Drucker said, "People don't follow policy; they follow people." Leadership is not a style we learn even though we can learn much about leadership, it is what one brings from inside to the position of leadership. It is an attitude of life that transforms into the core belief system of the school. Leaders provide the example for change and culture in an organization. As Albert Schweitzer said, "Example is not the main thing in influencing others … it is the only thing. I also like the quote by Frances Hodgson Burnett, "At first people refuse to believe that a strange new thing can be done, then they begin to hope it can be done, then they see it can be done—then it is done and all the world wonders why it was not done centuries ago." It is the belief in the impossible, the proving-the-world-wrong attitude that moves an organization. I observed this in the creation of Deerfield. We all had doubts. Can we really do this? Then came the hope in the dream and the reality of the creation over time. Finally this thought was with the staff: why isn't every center of learning like this?

A staff looks to their leader for reassurance and hope that we are on the right course for our school. From *The Art of Possibility,* authored by Rosamund Stone Zander and Benjamin Zander, comes this quote, "A leader is the relentless architect of the possibility that others can be." The leader helps staff maintain hope. "Maintaining hope comes from seeing the potential in every situation and staying positive despite circumstances." Leaders need to display a practical optimism. I received an e-mail from a Deerfield parent during a difficult time for our school which touched me and emphasizes this point. He expressed how much he admired me for being able to continue to be inspired by the children; to continue to put my best foot forward; to continue to run Deerfield the way it was being run; to continue to motivate the wonderful staff I was blessed with—all in the face of all the issues we were dealing with. I am thankful that that was what he was seeing, because there was a tremendous amount going on inside me that was much different. I have also had staff comment on my belief that all would turn out right and as it should. And I say, "Doesn't it?" Many times leaders communicate this on how they embrace change. "Change has a considerable psychological impact on the human mind. To the fearful it is threatening because it means that things may get worse. To the hopeful it is encouraging because things may get better. To the confident it is inspiring because the challenge exists to make things better," King Whitney Jr., from Laura Moncur's *Motivational Quotations.* The leader's confidence inspires staff to embrace the challenges of change and realize success. Success breeds success.

John C. Maxwell from *The Maxwell Leadership Bible* says, "People reflect their leader. We cannot expect followers to grow beyond their leader. We cannot expect followers to turn out fundamentally different from their leader." He talks about what a leader brings to the organization: attitudes, stability, compassion, honesty, and vision. All of these attributes form the foundation for the organization. When a leader fulfills his or her role in these areas, staff knows where they are going and are also supported in their role to connect the vision and attitude with their children. Dr. Parker Palmer said, "What we teach will never take unless it connects with the inward, living core of our students' lives, with our students' inward teacher." Creating culture is creating that living caring core that connects with the inward living core of students and their learning. The principal or director of the school sets the tone in school, and the teacher sets the tone in the classroom.

The teacher is the conveyer of the culture to the student. They model the culture. Students learn more from what we do than from what we say. "We need to be the people we want our children to become," says Rafe Esquith. I have had many students over the years talk to me about their teachers and the role they played in their lives. Children are very perceptive and can read adults. They know if they are genuine or putting on a front.

What do others look for in leaders? When I think of the great leaders through time—whether a leader of an organization, country, or a cause—people were drawn to them because of their passion. Through their passion they were able to move people toward a defined vision with consistency of purpose. They were the kind of people who are risk-takers. They shattered illusion. Daniel Boorstien says, "They are willing to try something that everyone thinks is outrageous and stupid." Gandhi said, "When you pursue your greatest passion, you will be amazed at who stands by your side." People follow passion. Think of leaders like Gandhi, Churchill, Kennedy, Lincoln, Mother Teresa, Truman, or Mandela. What drew people to them? They were passionate about what they were doing. They all dared to follow their heart even in the face of adversity. T.S. Eliot confirms this thought, "Only those who risk going too far can possibly find out how far one can go."

Leaders need to be dreamers and visionaries. They need to see the potential of an organization. These leaders have a high level of integrity choosing right over wrong, ethics over convenience, and truth over popularity. "Have the courage to say no. Have the courage to face the truth. Do the right thing because it is right. These are the magic keys to living your life with integrity," said W. Clement Stone. These people, leaders, measure their lives not by the world's standard of success, but by the fulfillment of their vision. "The future belongs to those who believe in the beauty of their dreams," said Eleanor Roosevelt. These leaders are selfless, not seeking acclaim for themselves but the success of what they believe in. Harry S. Truman said, "You can accomplish anything in life, provided that you do not mind who gets the credit."

There is also within these successful leaders a depth of integrity and sincerity in all they do. This is exemplified in what Dr. Martin Luther King Jr. said, referring to Gandhi's ability to make his will sincere in a speech he made in India, "If you ask people in India why is it that Mahatma Gandhi was able to do what he did in India, they will say they followed him because of his absolute sincerity…Any time he made a mistake, even in his personal life, or even a decision he made in the independence struggle, he came out in public and said, 'I made a mistake.'" How many leaders do we see in the world today who are willing to do this? I have personally found that saying you made a mistake has a tremendous healing effect on the staff and gives them a license to risk. I tell my staff every year they have freedom to fail. If they are not making some mistakes, they are not trying anything new. Organizations need risk-free zones where all staff can be themselves, take risks, fail, and be free to succeed. A risk-free zone is also where it is safe to say anything, question anything, and confront or challenge without repercussions. That creates a high level of trust, freedom, and empowerment. We all seek freedom. To find it, we need to balance our expectations with our reality. To create freedom and peace, we must strive for the balance. Leaders can give their staff space to realize this balance in their lives.

With leadership that exemplifies freedom, innovation, balance, and risk taking comes criticism, not all of which is constructive. Leaders who are different, visionaries, and trail blazers in their organizations will be criticized. I like Theodore Roosevelt's perspective on this.

> It is not the critic who counts, not the man who points out how the strong man stumbled or where

the doer of deeds could have done them better. The credit belongs to the man who is actually in the arena, whose face is marred by dust and sweat and blood; who strives valiantly; who errs, and comes short again and again, because there is no effort without error and shortcoming; who does actually try to do the deed; who knows the great enthusiasm, the great devotion and spends himself in a worthy cause; who, at the worst, if he fails, at least fails while daring greatly. Far better is it to dare mighty things, to win glorious triumphs even though checkered by failure, than to rank with those poor spirits who neither enjoy nor suffer much because they live in the gray twilight that knows neither victory nor defeat.

It is not the criticism that is important; it is how one responds to it. One needs to have a sense of humor about it and not take oneself too seriously. Leaders must be able to laugh at themselves. Equally important is not blocking out the criticism but listening to hear the facts, what is true. It may be an opportunity to learn something which will help one be better even though at the time it may be painful. Remember, leaders also should have freedom to fail. At least you are trying to make a difference. Rather than living in the gray twilight, as Roosevelt said, trail blazing leaders are daring greatly.

Successful leaders have a passion that helps an organization persevere toward a goal. Sir Winston Churchill said this in his speech to the boys of his public school in 1941, "Never give in—never, never, never, in nothing great or small, large or petty, never give in except to convictions of honor and good sense. Never yield to force; never yield to the apparently overwhelming might of the enemy." That is the kind of passion that wins wars and saves countries. That is the same kind of passion that turns organizations around.

Leaders with passion don't work to live; they live to do their work. Pablo Picasso says it better, "It is your work in life that is the ultimate deduction." People want to feel a part of what they do. Good leaders empower staff, encouraging them to use their talents to their fullest potential. John Quincy Adams said, "If your actions inspire others to dream more, learn more, do more and become more, you are a leader." Leaders give staff a sense of ownership of their organization through their involvement in the decision-making and development of the organization. It is done through the creation of a *we* culture. I like this statement from Charlotte Roberts from her book *Dance of Change*, "When I say 'I belong,' I don't mean that something possesses me, as a child would say, 'that belongs to me.' Rather I belong means I am a part of, intimately involved with something greater than myself. 'When I say I belong,' I mean here I am at home, and here I can become." Leaders embrace those with whom they work, helping them belong and feel at home in their organization.

This connectedness is what flows through an organization. It is what makes the culture successful. Warren Bennis said, "Good leaders make people feel that they're at the very heart of things, not at the periphery. Everyone feels that he or she makes a difference to the success of the organization. When that happens, people feel centered and that gives their work meaning." People want to feel a part of what they do. When the leader is connected with staff and the staff with students, all feel an integral part of the whole and there is ownership in the organization. All feel a high level of responsibility for the core values of the organization.

Three attributes of a leader that draw people to them and helps them feel an integral part of a school are genuineness, caring, and affirmation. People want to know that their leader truly cares for them not only for what they do on the job, but as a person. We live in a society that equates emotion with weakness. Showing one's emotions with one's staff can have a tremendous effect. It shows a genuineness and transparency that is reflected in the richness of an organization's culture.

Two ways genuineness can be shown are small acts of kindness and words of appreciation either written or spoken. It is as simple as asking about one's family or commenting on something one saw in a teacher's classroom. A simple e-mail of encouragement or appreciation has a tremendous effect. It is that encouragement when everything seems to be going wrong or one has self-doubts that is just what one needs to get us through. This reminds me of a quote by Albert Schweitzer that I have often reflected on, "In everyone's life, at some time our inner fire goes out. It is then burst into flame by an encounter with another human being. We should all be thankful for those people who rekindle the inner spirit." A leader can be the person who reignites the flame. I know I remember those great souls who have reignited my flame.

A staff should grow accustomed to their leader's care and affection, expressions of appreciation, and acts of kindness. No one is so important that he or she is above kindness. This aspect of leadership takes courage and confidence. This quote from Adam L. Gordon summarizes this point, "Life is mostly froth and bubble. Two things stand in stone. Kindness in another's trouble. Courage in your own."

The world does not need more bosses. It needs more leaders—servant-hearted souls to lead with sensitivity and true care and affection toward others. Our actions speak much louder than our words. If people know you love and value them, they'll go the extra mile for you.

I hope at Deerfield that I was able to fulfill my role as a leader. That my passion and love for children were always evident to students, parents, and staff. That my desire that all students reach their full potential and develop as a whole person was realized. And that my staff knew I truly cared for and supported them, and that they were fulfilled beyond their wildest dreams. If this happened, only then am I successful.

> Having taught for many years in another school, I'd always had a hole in my heart. Moving to Deerfield has been wonderful for me both professionally and personally. My connection to the children, staff, and parents I work with validates my reason for being a teacher. What is best for children is the very thing that motivates the people here. Embracing "Best Practices," honest to goodness reflection on learning, and not running from challenge is what the community of Deerfield is all about. The student benefits cannot be articulated clearly because the impact of this school goes well beyond the grade they are in. The commitment of this community as "Life Long Learners" is evident to anyone who comes to know us. Our enthusiasm is transmitted to all children who enter through the doors of Deerfield. I am grateful to have been welcomed into this culture of learning. The hole in my heart has been filled.
>
> Becky Purcell, third and fourth-grade teacher

"Outstanding people have one thing in common, an absolute sense of mission." Zig Ziglar

Our culture started with and continues to be our principal, Richard Njus! A leader creates leaders. Richard establishes an environment and a culture that gives us the freedom to take risks. He encourages and inspires staff members to find their inner strengths as individuals as well as educators. Deerfield Elementary School would never have become the school it is today without his positive leadership, his passion for teaching & learning, and his strong vision to create such a powerful working and learning environment for all.

The GreenHouse teachers have a mission to be the best leaders, teachers, teammates & friends. Together, we have big dreams, remarkable aspirations and are filled with goals for our students and for ourselves. We trust and help one another on a daily basis, and continually challenge one another to be the best we can be. The GreenHouse is a place where teachers are professionally developed every day. We are like a family working together toward a common goal of teaching our children academics, social skills and a shared responsibility for their character education.

One of the richest aspects that has been created for the children has been the feeling of connectedness to one another and to their teachers in the GreenHouse. The feeling of connectedness is shown not only through cooperation, but collaboration as well. All GreenHouse teachers take responsibility and are actively involved in the nurturing and development of all 120 children in our K-4 team. This powerful house connection allows *the children to take risks by putting them in an optimum learning environment where they feel safe to go beyond the normal expectations and succeed. The children take responsibility for their learning and feel capable to learn as much as they can with positive encouragement and continual support from all.*

We feel very fortunate and blessed to be a part of Deerfield!

Respectfully submitted by:

Kellie Slominski (Kindergarten)
Jill Armstrong (1/2 Teacher)
Beverly Hatcher (1/2 Teacher)
Penny Hamblin (3/4 Teacher)
Julee Henry (3/4 Teacher)
The GreenHouse Team

When I first decided to interview for a position at Deerfield, it was for all the wrong reasons. I wasn't too interested in "trying something new" or "working out of the box" as was advertised. I knew I could do those things and adapt to whatever was placed before me, but those were not my main objectives. My reasons were strictly personal and selfish: (1) I wasn't able to get a position back at my beloved Village Oaks, and (2) I thought it would make my personal life easier to have my own children at the same school I was teaching at. A third reason and an important one was that I always wanted to teach kindergarten and this was a chance to fulfill that dream.

So … I came into this adventure with what might have been the wrong attitude, but in seven years I can honestly say I have received far more from my experience than I could have imagined. Being a part of this school has changed me as a person. I have never worked so hard in my life. I have "morphed" into someone who wants and strives to "try something new" and "think out of the box." When you are surrounded by people that are constantly working toward a greater goal, you can not help but become a part of that.

My first principal once told me that "experience breeds intelligence," and I have never forgotten that. Everything I have experienced here, the good, the bad, and the ugly, has enriched my brain and my soul and made me a smarter and better person.

I have never liked change. I've always been perfectly content inside my warm and cozy "box." If something works, why fix it? At Deerfield we never seem to settle. Even when something works, why not see if we can improve upon it and make it even better? So, even though I like my comfortable box, I find myself always looking for a different way of doing something or a new way of presenting something. This is what this school and its culture has done for me.

I have many years ahead in my teaching career and although I may find myself somewhere other than Deerfield, I will be forever grateful for what this school, its principal, and its culture have done for me... made me a better person which in turn makes me a better teacher.

Cindy Lyon, kindergarten teacher

Chapter 10

Touching Hearts:
More Deerfield Family Stories

When Dr. Eric Glover, professor at East Tennessee State University, challenged me to write a book about the Deerfield experience, the first thought that came to my mind was how would I grasp and communicate the essence of the way the culture of Deerfield touched and changed the lives of those who experienced it. As I started writing the book and thinking of communicating our experience, I thought what better way to capture the thoughts about Deerfield than through a variety of testimonials from people young and old who daily passed through our doors, the Deerfield family.

This chapter is dedicated to hearts touched by the Deerfield experience. The next several pages contain a small portion of the many letters, cards, and e-mails I have received, sharing their experiences and insights into Deerfield. It was very difficult to choose which writings to place in the book. As I sat and read each contribution from my Deerfield family, many times with tears in my eyes, it brought back rich memories of a school that made a difference. From the bottom of my heart, I thank all who contributed and shared with me. It is my hope that these next few pages will touch you as they did me. More than that, they have captured the essence of the rich qualities of the culture of Deerfield.

It's impossible for me to express how I feel about the last seven years. As you know, the journey for me dates back about ten years to 1997 when I was on the cadre to develop Deerfield and then as Deerfield's first parent council president. This has been a journey, an experience that will stay with me and my family forever. Just one example is that my husband, Mike, and I never considered sending our oldest son to a private high school. We always thought that he would attend public high school. When he approached us three years ago and asked if we would consider letting him go to Catholic Central, I have to say that our Deerfield experience influenced our decision to send him there—at great financial sacrifice. Like Deerfield, Catholic Central feels like family. When someone is sick or dealing with a hardship, everyone comes together to help. The same thing happens again and again at Deerfield as you are well aware. I'll never forget when my father died (April 2004), and it was on the day of Family Fun Night (which I was chairing). Mike and I decided to come with Jack that evening, and we were overwhelmed with the love from you, Richard, the staff, and parents. Even some of Jack's peers who knew said nice things to him. It was the best decision to attend that event despite our sad loss because we were "with family."

So, to try to express how Deerfield has impacted

Richard L. Njus

our lives, I would have to say more than anything that the environment/culture feels like a family. It's overwhelming to feel that the staff and principal of your child's school are always right there at your side. It feels like we are not alone in this parenting journey. We feel like our child is wrapped up in the arms of everyone in the school whether it be the parent volunteers, the teachers, the custodians, the office staff or the principal. Prior to having a child at Deerfield, I had never seen children running up to hug a principal; I had never experienced a principal knowing every child's name in the building. Do you know how special that makes a child feel? Deerfield is a place where the principal's door is always open—no appointment necessary. Deerfield is a place where teachers give out their home phone numbers. Deerfield is a place where the slightest sign of bullying is immediately addressed and squashed. Deerfield is a place for every type of learner. Our first son to attend Deerfield was (is) a kinesthetic learner. This learning style was embraced at Deerfield and punished at his former elementary school. He is now an eighth grader and a 4.0 student who is happy and loves learning. Our second son to attend Deerfield (currently attending) hits his milestones about six months later than most of his peers because he was born premature and he has a summer birthday. His teachers understand him and make him feel good about his accomplishments. When he started kindergarten (based on pre-school experiences), he kept telling us he wasn't smart. Now he has confidence in himself.

I could go on and on. Deerfield has positively affected my family and so many others in countless ways! I am so thankful for these past seven years and will forever have the Deerfield family in my heart.

Cathy Reilly, parent and our
first president of our parent organization

As a Deerfield parent, I was proud to be a part of this phenomenal school. I want to express my appreciation for having had the opportunity to attend Deerfield for the past seven years. I am truly thankful to the NCSD for creating the opportunity for this phenomenal school. The entire experience has been such a wonderful privilege for our family. I love this school because of the administration, staff and teachers. The program is so enriched with the building blocks for strong character development. This positive reinforcement of respect and responsibility that my family has experienced at Deerfield will last a lifetime. We live the Deerfield pledge: "Deerfield Explorers are caring, responsible community members who respect themselves, others, and their environment"; not just my children, but my husband, Rob, and I live it as well. We have brought this commitment to character building into our home. We wouldn't be the family we are today, if it weren't for all the amazing teachers, staff, and principal at Deerfield. Richard Njus is a wonderful and caring educator. He believes in this school as many other parents do. We have been truly blessed to have had the opportunity to attend this amazing school for seven years and for that I am truly grateful!

Chris Aprilliano, parent

I like Deerfield because everyone is raspansabl incklooding me. And I have benn reading a lot and I have read 50 books this year. And I love having you as a pirisable at this school. I will always remember this school cuase I love reading and you make us read.

Sara, kindergartener in her own words

Deerfield Elementary School is very fortunate that I did not haul a tent into their school in 2001, pull up an old piece of log, and start playing guitar. They were also very fortunate that I didn't work my way into their kitchen and steal food from their refrigerator. And if you wish to ask me how to get anywhere within the building, I can tell you exactly what every door leads to. I know this school like the back of my hand. I know this school as if it was my own home, and I know it because I lived there. I experienced the culture from the inside out. I have felt its pulse, heard its sighs, drummed along with its beat and sang with its success.

In first grade, my six-year-old son had difficult issues and would not leave my side. My choice was to remain at school with him all day or be arrested for truancy! My little guy suffered from physical and emotional issues that negatively impacted his ability to remain without me in school. Full-day kindergarten went all right, but things kicked up a notch when we hit first grade, mostly due to a drug he was taking for his migraine headaches that increased his anxiety. We looked to Deerfield as a new beginning after his difficult baby days and toddlerhood. We never anticipated that I would not be able to leave the school grounds. As time went on, the anticipated professional counsel and a team approach to assisting our child proved to be a worthless hope … at first.

Over the course of four months, I sat all day at Deerfield waiting for my child to finish his school day. I had things that were not getting done at home and my two other young girls were being neglected because our son was demanding so much time and energy. My husband and I became very angry, first at the school and then at each other. Patience had turned to blame. We started to question whether we should pull him out of the school altogether. We were beginning to think that we had signed up for a very beautiful fancy building led by a cookie-cutter principal with an ego so large his office was too small to contain it. My back was aching from sitting on small chairs, I was hungry all the time, I was cold from not being able to move around and I was very, very lonely. This was not what I had envisioned when the last of my three children were finally in school full time. I was bored to tears, and it was agony to be ignored. Christmas came and went, and I was jealous of the teachers' comradeship. The hours ticked by. I waited and waited. And one particularly horrible day when my son acted very badly and a teacher finally acted slightly annoyed, I attempted to quit being a part of the "Deerfield family."

As I was spewing out disappointments and insults, the social worker looked at me calmly and said. "Okay, but you can't leave here mad…"and then she nodded toward the principal's office and said, "You owe it to him and to yourself to talk things out first." Something happened when I looked into the principal's office. I suddenly felt overwhelmed with pity. I felt deep pity for the principal; for his school, its misguided promises, and for the whole Novi Community School District who had worked so hard to establish this School of Choice.

Little did I know that the half-hour discussion I ended up having with the principal that day would change the course of my family's life forever. I tearfully sputtered my hateful opinion of his school, telling him we did not appreciate being considered a "dirty spot on Deerfield's clean, white apron." But his reaction surprised me. He calmly stretched out his legs, placed one foot over the other, rested his hands in his lap, and lightly shook his head. "No," he said, "you don't understand. It is all about love. We love all the children here. We care about all of them and their families. We love your child. We love your family. We love your son. We love Paul."

I sat there stunned. My argument was deflated. He had completely removed all my will to fight. He pulled out the wrong weapon! He had stolen all my reserve and ammunition that was cocked and ready to fire! I was speechless, defenseless, and I felt a strange feeling of being caught up in a safe net. Love was the last word I had expected to hear. I walked out that day feeling like the Grinch after a visit with little Cindy Lou Who. My heart had been more than two sizes too small.

Over the next three to four years, I watched Deerfield stay true to those words of love by introducing the concept of community and culture. The teachers' concern and support was effective. It allowed our family to relax and start working with what we had and not wishing for something we did not. If I had left the day I got angry, it would have been devastating to my family and affected the school community in ways I shudder to think about. Not only did my son make great strides in learning as time passed, my family healed and became stronger because the culture of the school, in essence, said:

"This is what we are going to do. We are going to walk together. We are going to listen to each other and hold each other in each other's heart. There will be rough times as well as good, and there will be days when you will have to apologize to us and days when we will have to apologize to you. And at the end of the time your child spends with us, he will have his dignity intact. He will have confidence in who he is, respect for others and above all else, an insurmountable love of learning."

I was so profoundly affected by our experience at Deerfield, I could not find the words to express my appreciation. In spite of myself, since I tend toward creative things, I created a logo for the school explaining our experience. As Murray Sidlin, conductor of the New Haven (CT) Symphony says, "When words are no longer adequate, when our passion is greater than we are able to express in a usual manner, people turn to art."

The logo depicts two people holding a small child between them in a heart. These two people can represent anyone, but for me they represent parents and teachers keeping the circle of community.

Elizabeth Copeland, parent

Daughter Lisa's thoughts (she is now in tenth grade): "I loved Deerfield because it was fun to enjoy all the age groups together. It felt like a huge pile of siblings. Like one great big family. It was never boring, we were not aware of our differences in our level of education. It was my best year ever… no one was involved in cliques. We had something going on called 'fads.' Fads were something we said all the time and even made the teacher join and laugh. One example is 'kitty horn' and since we all came from different schools when we joined Deerfield, we accepted each other unconditionally. On the last day, in commemoration of our good times we had a student-led little ceremony on the playground and buried crackers in the wood chips. Someone probably said a speech like, 'In memory of our last day of Deerfield, here lies the leftover crackers from so-and-so's lunch.' It was a great year for me, I came in not knowing what to expect and left feeling like I had been a part of building something great."

Daughter Chantal's thoughts (she is now in eighth grade):
"I loved Deerfield. I remember when the music started to play we would get really excited because it was time to gather in the project area for a learning activity. It was our chance to get together with all the kids in our house from different grade levels. I loved the fact that we all ate together at lunch and helped the kids with their meals and their snow gear. There was never an issue of who was in what level. We were all just learning together."

Son Paul's thoughts (he is now in sixth grade):
"I loved the socializing at Deerfield between all grades. I liked being able to help the younger ones and have the older kids help me. The teachers were great and we could learn at our own pace. I liked that we could move around during the day. I never felt left behind."

Richard L. Njus

Deerfield is the best school in the whole world. I wouldn't have it any other way. Novi schools are redistricting. This resulting in a Giant HOLE IN THE PROCESS OF ELEMENTARY SCHOOLS!!!

Andrew third grade

My name is Kim Giroux. My husband, Bill, and our family have had the blessed experience of being a part of the Deerfield family throughout our children's entire elementary years. This in itself is amazing because of the lottery system placed at the school's conception and the recent changes the school has had to adapt to based on the board and city officials viewpoints. We were one of the "lucky" families who slipped in between two challenging obstacles. This alone is not the reason we have been lucky. We know God had us in an amazing place during some very difficult years in our lives and especially in the lives of our children.

As Kathryn entered kindergarten, I was diagnosed with Hodgkin's Lymphoma. I was told that it was very curable, but it was still difficult having a five-year-old and a three-year-old and enduring the tiring days and months of chemotherapy. It was also stressful on Kathryn as her teacher's husband passed away of "cancer" during my treatment. The word "cancer" now took on a whole new meaning. Although this time was difficult it was nothing compared to what was to come. Six months after treatment, it was back. This time the chances for recovery dropped to 30% and I would have to endure a stem cell transplant.

All eyes and attention totally came off our two beautiful daughters and were focused on my survival.

I found the courage to write a letter to the staff of Deerfield not only explaining our situation, but giving detailed descriptions and needs of each of my children. "Krystina (now five and in kindergarten) needs lots of physical reinforcement in the form of hugs and touches. Kathryn (now seven) does not express her emotions but is hurting deeply." I poured my fears and heart out on to the pages. After all, if we ever needed a "village" to help raise our family, it was now.

What happened next was amazing. The troops were rallied. Mr. Njus sent out a letter reminding parents to keep their children home if they were ill; explaining that a parent in the school needed extra support in this area for health reasons. (After all, a simple cold could ultimately end my life.) The teachers were diligent about teaching the kids to cough into the crook of their elbows. The office staff was loving and patient, nurturing repeated "tummy aches" and "boo boos" for the girls and for making exceptions for my handicapped mother for pick-ups and drop-offs. Mrs. Riley (art teacher) made special days after school (during my month-long hospitalization) for the girls to come make special projects for me and for themselves. What fun! Krystina still talks about the hug that our music teacher, Mrs. Sonntag, gave her right in the middle of class because she was crying and missing me. Even Mr. Bunker (the custodian) made extra attempts to talk to my children and brighten their day with his kind words and enthusiasm. Kathryn's Deerfield Girl Scout troop got together and had the families make meals for all of us so we would have a few more moments away from daily tasks, to enjoy time together. They also sent a Christmas tree full of homemade ornaments to the hospital for me. What pride and love I saw on Kathryn's face, through the glass wall that separated us, when she delivered it to me. It seemed as though every inch of Deerfield was pouring itself into our children and our family. It was very evident that the philosophy of the school was about growing the whole child. And that sometimes academics are not only what is required to help a child learn. If a child's emotional or spiritual level is not filled up, the child cannot learn. Deerfield staff not only understood this, they took action to make sure that our children were well cared for on every level.

Yes, cancer is a blessing, for all of the reasons mentioned above and many, many more. Deerfield picked up where we couldn't. During this time our children did not have parents. (Thank God for Grandma.) But we knew that most of their day was spent with caring women and men at Deerfield Elementary who sincerely were making every effort to teach our kids through example. Deerfield became their family. Deerfield your statement is bold: nurture, support, and love the whole child, and a child will grow—abundantly! I know that there were many other instances and details that went unnoticed and were done out of silent love and compassion for our family and the welfare of each of our girls. We are eternally grateful to Deerfield, the neighborhoods of families, and churches that surrounded us. It truly does take a village. I am so glad that Deerfield was in our village!

Kim Giroux, Parent

Mr. Njus is my favorite friend out of all my friends.
Deerfield is Happy Place for kids.

Daniel, second grade

Deerfield is a special place because there are nice people here.
You get a lot of education too.

Angelo, first grader

Richard L. Njus

Dear Mr. Njus,

So, as other parents, I will begin my story.

As you know, my experience with Deerfield began last spring with the open house for new kindergarten parents for the 2006–07 school year. My first thoughts, "What a school!"

This tour was then followed by the orientation of parents chosen to attend Deerfield in the fall. You were quite the speaker that night. I listened to your words and had so much admiration for your commitment to Deerfield and the children. I had worked in an environment to which I heard many a man speak (automotive industry), but only one other man, my pastor, came even close to your true expression of commitment to your cause, that which is Deerfield Elementary.

Between your thoughts, then meeting the teachers and the question/answer period to which every question was listened to and answered, I was amazed. I had heard only positive things about Deerfield, since moving to Novi the past few years, but that night, I not only saw through my own eyes the uniqueness of the facility itself, but the extraordinary teaching style you and the staff strive to achieve.

I walked out with such excitement for my children. I felt honored to now become part of the Deerfield family. Most important to my heart, blessed that my children would begin their academic careers at Deerfield Elementary.

My story now begins to differ from a great many others who may have written to you with their thoughts about Deerfield. My writing goes to a deeper personal level. As my son, Ryan, began his journey into kindergarten, he had more than just going into kindergarten issues: he had the issue of his precious health.

My son, Ryan, as you know, was born with a congenital heart defect Tetra logy of Fallot. When he was born, he had two holes is in heart, and his pulmonary artery was tightening as he grew, causing his blood oxygen to be at extremely low levels. The babies are often termed "blue babies." There was a bluish tint to the early pictures of Ryan.

The worst of blue spells occurred while he was alone in my care. It happened in his first year of life. His pulse oxygen level was as low as 66%, normal level to be 95–100%, when he was rushed to the University of Michigan for complete open heart surgery. Had that afternoon occurred thirty some years ago, Ryan would not be with us. To be even more honest, even now, children who have had their hearts repaired do not make it past milestones in their lives. I will be honest that thought is my life and fear everyday.

Since his repair, he is no longer blue. His heart is monitored on a regular basis. Although his is now limited in activities, such as contact sports, and tires very easily. Ryan tries to be just a regular kid. At his age now, he knows no one should touch his chest; he needs to sit when he gets winded, and really watches the choices he makes on a daily basis.

So, as my firstborn was becoming a kindergartner, I explored both schools in our district. Deerfield, liking the all day kindergarten curriculum, and then a half-day school, which his doctor preferred for his first year in academics.

Because of Ryan's doctor's concerns, I checked out the half-day school while really wanting Deerfield. My decision was not one of just a choice between all day and half-day school. My decision was about Ryan's life and health. I know most would think over protective mom, but I believe I have earned that title.

As it happened four years ago, I had to give him to those surgeons for hours; I was now going to give him up to the hands not only the kindergarten staff, but the entire elementary staff.

Ryan's cardiologist was adamant at first that Ryan would be to tired for all day kindergarten, but I wanted him in all day, because all day meant Deerfield.

I did explore all the options. This part of my story is one I have not told. Just as Deerfield had an open house, so did the other schools in the district for half-day kindergarten. I walked into our neighborhood school at that time and had a true sense of fear. There were children everywhere in the halls, with it seemed, no direction? Worry came over my whole body. I walked out physically ill. I sat in my car and wept tears of fear for Ryan. He would walk in just another kindergartner, and that would be it. He would be lost in the school, completely lost. Just another kindergartner, but in Ryan's case, it is not about just his learning, it is about his life. I was scared to the core my child may lose his life in such a harried environment.

With this story and my feelings about Deerfield being the complete opposite of what I saw that day, I convinced Ryan's doctor to change her mind. She would allow me to give him a chance by educating you Mr. Njus and Mrs. Lyon, his teacher of his capabilities, tendency to try to keep up with others he may not be able to physically do, and his tiredness, that he would sit and rest if he had to. I promised and owed it to Ryan to let everyone know at Deerfield what my concerns were.

So as I should have expected, you and your staff were incredible. You listened to Ryan's needs and my fears. My fears, he may be cast aside during things he can't do. His safety at recess. His physical health later on in the school day.

But there you were saying, "We will work this out." And work it out you and your staff did. Mrs. Lyon I know watches him with a mother's eye. Mrs. Snow adores him and is sure to limit his physical actions during gym class. And I think all of you put together the plan for Ryan to have his own special computer work station in the library when Mrs. Snow has an activity on her schedule that Ryan can't do. He won't be just a kid on the side doing sit ups. He will just be excelling more in an activity he actually loves, the computer!

Ryan's doctor is amazed at Deerfield. I received an okay as long as we watched over him. I say we because not only me, Mr. Larry, our bus driver, accommodates Ryan, he need only walk to the driveway, Mrs. Snow accommodates with computer station seven from the wonderful Mrs. Canady, the lunchroom ladies, the recess ladies, and especially you, Mr. Njus.

The second Ryan walked in, my concerns were listened to, acknowledged, and a plan was made that took action. The perfect strategic model for a successful academic life.

I am completely convinced that if Ryan was unable to attend Deerfield, my choice would have had to be a private school at all costs. Deerfield's ability to accommodate Ryan was what a private school could accomplish, and a school with the curriculum that we all grew up with could not. I believe he would have just been another new kindergarten, and I would have been an overbearing mother. I consider Deerfield, our private school, place in a public school system.

My positive experience with Ryan and Deerfield even touches my own health as a parent. Could it be because I am a Deerfield family member? Absolutely!

I was considered disabled in Ryan's first years of life. I developed severe painful Rheumatoid Arthritis and Lupus these last years. I am a stay-at-home mom, by choice, but also by default due to my health. I have my good days and bad.

What does this have to do with Deerfield? Probably emotionally the best thing to happen to me as I am in this mom-thing. Volunteering to help at Deerfield is not a burden to me; it is my wish. And every time I sign up to assist in anything, Mrs. Lyon knows without saying I need a place to sit; she makes sure I can still be that kind of Mom I want to be. I wonder if she knows what that means to me. Other women with my disease may sit at home and hurt. With Deerfield as my motivation, I get up some days just for that little amount of times I can feel important again. Useful. Needed.

Then the one day, I will never forget. You, Mr. Njus, helped me emotionally. You may not remember those first few days when I left Ryan and cried. You said to me, "You know you can have lunch with him anytime." Out went my fears; you mean I could see him on those days when my illness takes over and I feel sorry for myself. Or when Ryan's heart weighs heavily on my mind. Those kinds of days are the worst, but when I get up and decide to have lunch with him, my whole attitude of self-pity goes away. Never in any academic facility had I heard that I could be a part of school hours. Even after school activities discourage too much parental involvement. Your encouragement to make it a part of my day helped me and Ryan!

So, as you know, I am often in the lunchroom talking to the kids or Mrs. Lyon has set up the most comfortable place in an open activity to be a helping Mom, but with my limitations.

Now I have my number two child, Emma, (adopted from Russia at fifteen months) to be in kindergarten fall 2007. I know as anyone reads this, they must think this can't happen to one family, but there is more. Emma was diagnosed recently with Reactive Attachment Disorder and severe brain damage caused by extreme alcohol exposure during her fetal development. She is in our school system's preschool program and recently began to show some of the common side effects of these two disorders. But, I keep thinking, when she gets to Deerfield, she will get the help she and I both need. I admit to be a praying Christian, and this last week was a tough one with behavior issues at home. I stepped away, knelt down, and prayed for the next seven months to go by quickly. What happens in seven months? Then she will be taking her first steps at Deerfield.

You and your staff have already showed me the amount of extra care you give out. The best for Emma will be Deerfield. I already have spoken to Mrs. Lyon, and we are planning a meeting in the spring with all the evaluations, and the IEP received this school year. Mrs. Lyon is already showing the extra interest that may be needed. Deerfield's philosophy is so proactive. Emma won't walk into a class where the teacher isn't interested until something happens. I hope to bring enough to the table that Mrs. Lyon and you have all the information you want to help her succeed.

As I now will close, let me tell you how Deerfield and your staff has gone way beyond my imagination in helping Ryan, myself, and I am sure for Emma. This is no ordinary elementary school.

I am a true believer in prayer. Please know Deerfield is in my prayers everyday. I know what a privilege it is to be a Deerfield family, and I thank the Lord every day Ryan steps on that bus, I help with the Lighthouse fun, or I look around that lunchroom and see all those precious ones. My prayer is everyone in the Deerfield family feels the same. Because, Mr. Njus, if that is the case, you are remarkable!

On a lighter note, as I conclude, I mentioned to Ryan I was writing to you about Deerfield. He said to tell you, "Deerfield is fantastico!" I think that sums it all up.

My best to you and all the staff,

Patricia Greenwald, parent

I like Deerfield because the teachers take time to work with you. I like how when I come to school, Mr. Njus is at the door and says hi to you. When I came to Deerfield in kindergarten, I was scared, but I knew that my brother, Taylor, was more scared than me. He had been at a different school, and now he had to start over. Everyone made us feel welcome, and by the second day we weren't scared anymore.

I liked how I could see my brother a lot when I was at school. He ate lunch in the lunchroom at the same time as me and had lunch recess the same as me. We did this thing on Fridays called "family groups," and because he's my real family, he was in my group. So were some other kids that were brother and sister. Sometimes we would make stuff together. One time we made a giant paper snowman, and each person in our family group got to make a part of it. I got to make the hat and Taylor made the body. It was fun. I liked being able to see my brother during the day and know that he's there if I am lonesome. But now Taylor is in seventh grade, and I won't be at the same school as him again.

I love Deerfield. Thank you for my great report card and all you've done for me.

Alicia, third grader

Deerfield is special because Everybodys learning. Your dentrites grow. In Deerfield everyone has to be responsible.

Nimalan, second grader

It was the late 1990s, and I volunteered to sit on a committee, where we discussed elementary education and gave feedback on current experiences, as well as dreams and goals for the future for our kids in Novi. I liked the experience, and I didn't realize that what the committee continued to work on, became my children's new school, Deerfield Elementary. I can most adequately describe Deerfield as "all the best of what I remember from my own elementary school and, at the same time, is all the best of what is new and educationally valuable today."

My K-6 school was less than a mile away, and we walked, even home for lunch. There was a great emphasis on teaching and not just from the textbook. We had outdoor learning and nature trails in the woods, where older students were tour guides for groups from other schools. The first mainstreaming of special needs children happened in our school, and we paved some of the trails to accommodate wheelchairs. We also had a principal who cared deeply for the students and called them by name. He shared his family's summer adventures of mountain climbing through slide shows at school. It was an exciting place to learn.

The same can be said for Deerfield Elementary—it's an exciting place to learn. We have a wonderful principal, Mr. Richard Njus, who has a personal connection with the students, as well as strong leadership of staff with respect, discipline, and integrity. Mr. Njus values diversity, character-building, multiple-intelligences, and shares his experiences and educational priorities. He continues to keep learning himself, which helps our community to continue to improve. I have really enjoyed his newsletter and parents have a tremendous resource, as he shares articles of interest regarding children, school, parenting, and family values.

In 2000, we had two children at Parkview and had to decide whether to move over to Deerfield. We chose to keep our eldest at Parkview for his last year and move our daughter to Deerfield. Our reasons for choosing Deerfield were as follows: it is close to our home and we enjoy biking to school on nice days. The concept of education was clearly well-researched and implemented the best practices. The principal was Christian and the staff supported his positive direction. We liked the "one room schoolhouse" concept as well as having a teacher for two years.

There were a lot of little things, but it came down to seeing a principal, staff and families who all wanted something special. It was so obvious that first year that everyone loved being there, staff and students alike. The staff was full of enthusiasm, love of learning, care, positive discipline and encouragement of all students. We could tell that our children would be seen as a whole child, not just the quiet one, or the one behind in reading. No matter what, the teachers would be positive and encouraging of the students, even the most challenging ones. I loved hearing the teacher say, "no, we don't do that here at Deerfield." The kids seemed to live up to the high expectations staff had of them for education and behavior.

Those reasons we chose Deerfield are all still reasons we love it today. We have two more children attending now, and they continue to benefit from Deerfield's very professional and talented staff and are getting a great education. The Deerfield pledge is lived out by staff, students, and parents and a cooperative community is the wonderful result.

BettyJane Blossfeld, parent

Deerfield is special because it is not like other schools. It has multi-age so that we could get along with people.
Varsha, third grader

My Experience at Deerfield
I started at Deerfield when the school first opened and enjoyed every moment of every year. It was basically my "home away from home." When I went back every year, there was never any stress or anxiety because you knew what was expected of you, and you knew the

environment and the staff. There was always something to look forward to, and there was a very happy environment at Deerfield. There was always a smiling face there to greet you when you walked into the classroom. The teachers knew your strengths and weaknesses and they challenged you every step of the way. The Deerfield pledge states, "Deerfield explorers are caring responsible community members who respect themselves, others, and their environment." This pledge is completely true. All the kids that go to the school treat it like they would treat their home (when their parents are home) ☺. Every day was different and exciting, and I loved every moment of it. I wish that I still went to Deerfield… in fact, as a middle school student I still go back every week as a volunteer and everybody knows my name and makes me feel as welcome as when I was a student there!

Unsh Thakore
seventh grade
Novi Middle School

Deerfield is a special place, because it has beautiful teachers in this school. And the kids are happy a lot. Just like me! Special because everyone is kind to other kids. And what great books we have! I have a great time. It is so much fun.

Love, Emma, third grader

My son doesn't fit in a box. We found that out in preschool. He would cry at night about school the next day. At drop off in the morning he would hold on to me, cry, and refuse to get out of the car. The private preschool he attended told us that it was our parenting, that he needed a nanny, that they could not "handle" him more than half-a-day. So it was with much trepidation that we enrolled him, the next year, in kindergarten at Deerfield Elementary. After all, he had struggled in a Montessori program. How was this going to be any different? We held our breath, waiting each day for Deerfield to discover that they couldn't "handle" him either. We waited and waited and waited. My son is now in second grade, and we have never received the call we so surely believed would come. I've realized in hindsight that, while my son can be a handful, he did not feel liked and supported for who he was at preschool and felt this deeply. Deerfield has embraced him but not so tightly that he can't express who he is. He loves school now, and he loves his teachers. Most importantly he feels loved in such a powerful way that it defies written description. He has grown from a fragile child filled with confusion and fear of rejection to a confident learner who does not feel a moment of hesitation as I send him off to school every morning. This is the gift Deerfield has given him. It is priceless.

Name withheld, parent

As an educator for 20+ years, I have always been proud to be part of the public education system. "Schools of choice" were really not an option for my children or me. I live in the Farmington Hills Michigan school district. They decided to open an elementary school of choice which they called Highmeadow. I listened with interest how they were delivering curriculum and their approach to children's social and emotional well-being. Their program was extremely unique in the fact that children had elective classes they could choose from. But still I went back to thinking that so far the public education at Forest Elementary was just fine for my children.

A defining moment happens in most people, and from that instance, you know things will never be the same. That moment for me came when my son was in first grade, and in April he just read. I don't mean reading, I mean he was reading everything, and it was way above grade level, and he knew it and so did I. Michael had mentioned that there were three "special" students who got to read in above-grade-level books in his class, and he wanted to join them. Well, when I made an appointment with his teacher, she expressed to me that it was late in the year to move anyone and that if he were to be moved he needed to finish his book and read the advance material too. I was totally confused! Was it a punishment to excel? Why does he have to do double the amount of work? And is this the attitude of regular public schools? This had become my defining moment. On a whim that year, I had put Michael's name in the lottery for Highmeadow. Now I was convinced that if I won the "lottery" a place at Highmeadow for him we were definitely taking it. That June I did hear and Michael had been placed at Highmeadow. After the first week my son's response to his new school was, "Do I ever have to go back to that old school? Because I don't ever want to go back."

At this same time, Novi was exploring the possibility of a "school of choice" for their district. I immediately called the administration office and got on the study committee. Once the committee decided the direction, they were going, I helped plan the design for the building. I was also on the planning for the curriculum and how it would be delivered. I even had the privilege to be involved in the last interview for the principal of the new school. Once hearing Richard Njus speak, I knew right then and there I wanted to teach at that school.

During the building phase, I went each week in the summer to see the progress of the building. I could feel it in my bones that this school was somewhere special to teach. August just couldn't come fast enough. To this day, after seven years working at Deerfield, I still remember the special feeling I had walking in that building being part of something new in Novi. The assembly that first day verified my feelings. There was electricity in the air. As I stood in the gym feeling the community atmosphere literally building before my eyes I knew I made the right decision to be part of this. I had never worked harder in all my life that year, and yet it just felt like fun and invigorating. And then the "icing on the cake" came when Richard asked me to take a very special student. He was troubled because of his genius and seemed to be misunderstood. I was very touched that Richard had thought so much of me and felt I could make a difference with that child. I believe the reason I could do that was that Richard had empowered his teachers to make decisions and know that they might fail, and that was alright. This student and I went through some trying times, to say the least but by the time he left I knew I could count on him to make a significant contribution to the world.

Deerfield Elementary is like no other place. A sense of community, and caring are apparent as you enter the building. I have worked in five other buildings and I have never felt such a belonging as I do here. There is a joy to come to work everyday, because you know that through Richard's leadership, the most important thing in that building are the children. Making a difference each day in their lives, is what it is that school is all about. At Deerfield, the policy is no child is ever left behind. My only regret is that I am near the end of my career and eventually will miss getting up to spend my days at Deerfield.

Julie Kaufman,
Deerfield 3–4 teacher

Our two children, Rebecca and Michael, have both attended Deerfield Elementary.

We reside from England and moved to the USA in 2000. With the UK education system being different to the USA age wise (4–16 verses 5–18), we wanted Rebecca and Michael to both stay ahead as much as they could in case we had to return home. Deerfield at the time was the only school in Novi to have full-day kindergarten for Michael. Rebecca decided herself to move to Deerfield after a visit to the school and liking it so much.

Deerfield is a very caring school. You feel the warmth of the atmosphere from the second you walk in the door. Every member of staff are so dedicated to helping our children grow both academically and socially. Staff, students, and parents have respect for one another and are willing to help each other in any way they can. They have all become our extended family whatever their nationality.

Every time I visit the classroom to volunteer I see the children always so eager to learn and they are having fun at the same time. We couldn't ask for a better school for our children to develop and to grow into respectful young adults.

Sharon and Julian Sherborne

A quote from Michael: "The best thing about Deerfield is having the best principal and teachers to help me learn."

A quote from Rebecca: "I loved the working environment at Deerfield. I had fun while learning. I liked having my brother close in the same house."

Chapter 11

Prophecy Fulfilled, Dream Denied

"I am sad when I see so many good teachers and parents surrender to forces that sap their potential excellence.

Those who care deeply often feel outgunned by apathetic or incompetent administrators and politicians.

Expectations for children are ridiculously low."

Rafe Esquith

Through the years, the approval rating for Deerfield continually grew. Outside our school district, we were held up as a model of best practices and innovation. We had many educators come to tour and learn from our staff. Some spent days in classes and with staff. We helped many educators in the development and establishment of many programs in their schools. It was a joy to share our expertise and materials with other educators. This was very fulfilling for staff and helped them in their professional growth as teachers and as leaders. Our school also became a place where many colleges and universities wanted to place their interns and student teachers. We became a true learning community.

Our parents were very excited about partnering in their children's education. They felt an integral part of our school. More and more parents tried to get their children into Deerfield. I had monthly tours of interested parents, and we had to hold lotteries every year when filling open spaces for students because the number of applicants was so high. I received calls from around the United States and many countries from people moving into the Detroit area and desiring to send their children to Deerfield. Deerfield stayed at capacity.

As the success and the popularity of our school increased, the jealousy, judgment, and questioning about Deerfield increased. Parents who were not a part of Deerfield were unhappy that they could not get into Deerfield. We heard many statements like "Deerfield has this. Why doesn't my school have that?" All schools in our district have the same budget. We made different choices on where to spend our funds. Whereas outside our district Deerfield was held up as a model school; inside our district, ridicule, judgment, and anger toward Deerfield arose. Most of this was due to misinformation and misperceptions. The school district board of education and upper level administration began receiving questions and comments about Deerfield and the whys. Why do we do what we do? Why doesn't my school have this or that? Why can't we all have what they have? And on and on. The atmosphere in the district became quite divisive. I feel this could have been handled with clear, open communication from our school board and district leadership. But there began a push to do away with Deerfield's magnet school designation and the desire to make it a neighborhood school. This would, as was said frequently, "make us all the same."

In 2005 our school board began a discussion of redistricting our school district to relieve the over crowding in our elementary schools and to prepare for future growth in our community. Within this discussion arose the recommendation to make Deerfield a neighborhood school. This grew out of a feeling that there was competition and contention among the elementary schools in the district. One board member said Deerfield should be made into a neighborhood school to alleviate the divisiveness in the district over Deerfield. The board talked about all elementary schools being the same, and that by changing Deerfield to a neighborhood school, it would break down the comparisons and bad feelings.

When I heard these statements, it brought to mind the statement by Dr. Parker Palmer in the fall of 2001, "You are a satellite and they will try to pull you back into traditionalism." The dream of a magnet school, maintaining and improving our program, and keeping choice for our community was in jeopardy. That decision would impact 350 students at Deerfield and negate the concept of a magnet/school of choice for the school district. It would also cause tremendous disruption to the program and development of our school. Having 350 new students and parents who may not buy in to the program the school had developed would be like starting all over again. We would be working with parents to help them understand the differences between our program and the program in the school they were coming from and starting over to create our culture with a new student body.

To say the least, Deerfield parents were very frustrated and angry and felt that the promise they had been given for our school was being denied. And as I said to the school board the night they made their decision, it sent a message as to our standing as a forward-thinking, trail-blazing district in the area. Our parents felt the same way. I had many discussions with parents. They felt that through a concerted effort with reliable facts and research they would be able to change the board's mind. I encouraged our parents to be professional in all they did. I told them that they were role models for their children. They needed to model the pledge their children said every day, "Deerfield Explorers are caring responsible community members who respect themselves, others and their environment." I can say with pride that in the year that parents tried to present their proposals, information, and recommendation to the board, they conducted themselves in a highly professional manner. Their children can be proud of how their parents conducted themselves.

There were parents at every board meeting, presenting their concerns and recommendations. We had district school board meetings which ran to all hours of the night. One meeting had more than two hundred people in attendance. Our longest board meeting ended at 2:15 a.m. Parents stood in line for more than two hours to speak, each limited to five minutes to present. Our parents gathered information, research from university studies, Web sites, and from school districts that had magnet schools from all over the United States. The parents spoke to a superintendent from north of Chicago whose district had gone through the same issue with a magnet school. He volunteered to come and share with our school board. He told our parents that he did not make their magnet school a neighborhood school because of the merit it brought to the school district, but instead added more magnet schools to the school district.

The information our parents gathered overwhelmingly

supported magnet schools in districts that were on the leading edge, trail blazers in education. To give you a partial understanding of the extent to which parents went to change the school board members' minds, I have included the following proposal that a committee of Deerfield parents presented to the school district board at an open board meeting.

Deerfield Community Council
Parent Task Force

Magnet School and Novi Community School District Data

January 26, 2006
Report Prepared for the
Novi Community School District Board of Education
Task Force Members:

Linda Boran	Vicki McLeod	Erin Ryan
Linda Conroy	Bobbie Murphy	Marcy Salemi
John Cotter	Dawn O'Connor	Michael Salemi
Alison Dolin	Karen Quinn	Richelle Schultz
Alice Elkin	Audrey Racicot	Julie Silberg
Homero Hinojosa	Beverly Robson	Kathy Takeshita
Ram Krishnamurthy	Cheryl Roest	Kang-Lee Tu
Christine Luongo-Gordon	Nisha Rushton	Kelle Vela

Magnet School and Novi Community School District Data

The DCC Is Supporting the Continuation of Deerfield as a Magnet School

Introduction

In recent weeks, families of the Novi Community School District have been made aware of the Board of Education's and Administration's desire to redistrict the elementary schools. Parameters of the redistricting include that "every elementary school will be a neighborhood school and have its own attendance area"—a parameter that would change Deerfield Elementary School from a Magnet school attracting children and families throughout the District and impacting almost 90% of its present attendees.

Because of the swiftness of the proposed change, the Deerfield Community Council and concerned parents of Deerfield Elementary School formed an ad-hoc Task Force to collect data and facts supporting Deerfield as a magnet school. This data is intended to create awareness of what the community has at stake in Deerfield and to bring to light that such a monumental change deserves a level of research and analysis comparable to that which went in to creating Deerfield in 1998.

Richard L. Njus

Overview

Data collected includes the following and is tabbed at the end of this report:

1. ***Report from the Innovative Elementary School Cadre Study***— This document summarizes the process that was followed and the findings of 25 committee members representing parents, the community, teachers and administration, that was the definitive document the district used to create Deerfield. It was not about a building, it was about a vision for innovative education.

2. ***Cost Data***—This section covers cost data for elementary schools as provided from the District.

3. ***MEAP Scores***—This section contains a high-level summary of MEAP scores for Novi's elementary schools.

4. ***DCC Spending***—This section summarizes the DCC's financial contributions to Deerfield intended to enrich the lives of our children's educational experience.

5. ***Magnet Schools Research***—This section contains a summary of findings from Internet research of magnet schools throughout the country and extrapolations of that information as it relates to Novi. Selected research documents have also been included.

6. ***Magnet School Interviews***–This section contains several summaries of Magnet school programs in nearby districts

Conclusions

1. Report from the Innovative Elementary School Cadre Study—Our conclusion is that the District spent an enormous amount of time through the efforts of a dedicated group of parents and educators to come up with a "best practices" solution as an innovative approach to elementary education. At the time of the project's inception, there was no physical building for such a program. The conclusions reached from this study included adopting many educational concepts already in place throughout the district, including things such as looping, but also introducing newer concepts such as early-elementary foreign language instruction and full-day kindergarten.

A school bond issue was passed, an experienced educator and administrator was hired to oversee the project, the new school was built and named Deerfield, and the school was quickly populated with students. Today of course it is at capacity, and in demand with a long waiting list. This fact alone should be an indicator to the Board that Deerfield is highly regarded among elementary school families in Novi.

The Task Force asks that if this successful program is slated to be fundamentally changed, that prior to any change, another study similarly endowed be conducted to determine if best-practices or other education-based reasons exist (other then financial or redistricting related) to warrant the change; in other words, if something has changed in the educational practices arena that would mandate a different conclusion than the Cadre study.

2. Cost Data—Among the most prevalent misconceptions about Deerfield is that it costs more to run than the other schools; and that this cost provides an unfair advantage to those that attend, with a commensurate disadvantage to other elementary school children.

The data shown here, provided by the Novi Community School District, indicates that Deerfield's operating costs are not only in line with those of the other schools, but rather *Deerfield operates at the lowest cost per student of all the elementary schools in our district.* It should be noted that *all of the schools* operate in a reasonably tight cost band that does not vary by more than about $200,000, or less then 10% of the average operating cost of elementary schools in our district. (This analysis excludes funding specifically for Special Education.)

It should also be noted that the total cost per student figure for Deerfield *includes* the busing costs which have been specifically mentioned as an item of concern.

An in-depth review of this data will reveal other conclusions, such as the cost per student at each school moving with changes in its enrollment. For example—if Parkview enrollment goes down, its cost per student will increase and if Village Oaks enrollment goes up, its cost per student will go down; thus redistricting of any type will affect these numbers.

3. MEAP Scores—MEAP scores are a tool that Michigan school districts use to measure academic achievement and "AYP" or adequate yearly progress—a task mandated by the "No Child Left Behind Act." On a composite basis, Deerfield has the highest MEAP scores of all the elementary schools. However, a breakdown of the composite scores into its components reveals that other schools score higher, lower and about the same as Deerfield.

The Task Force parents are not educators and thus are not equipped to provide detailed analysis of the true meaning of absolute and year to year MEAP scores. Our district's teachers and educators are skilled in this area.

We can conclude, however, that there is no academic failure of Deerfield as an elementary school thus no academic reason for making a fundamental change in how students attend this school.

4. DCC Spending—The DCC is our PTO. Strong parental involvement results in important and meaningful contributions to the school. Our DCC has provided the school with many different contributions such as a rock-climbing wall, playground equipment, books, and other long lasting items. The DCC also contributes money to each teacher to help them supply their own classroom.

While we have no metric in which to measure our PTO, either by itself or in relation to other schools, we all know that our DCC is very strong and makes Deerfield a better school with each passing year.

5. Magnet Schools Research—Cursory analysis of this research tells us just how unique Novi's magnet school is. Many magnet schools are thematic-based; ours is best-practices. Many have admission policies based on some achievement measure; ours is open by lottery. Many were created to achieve some form of social, racial or economic equality; our diversity falls out of our random lottery process. Many have been funded with special Federal or State funds that support magnet school programs, racial integration or busing programs, or similar; Deerfield has received no such funds.

No matter how you measure it, we appear to have a unique

and successful program. Families are at Deerfield by choice and not default. With that in mind, our conclusion is why choose to make a fundamental change to a successful program?

6. Magnet School Interviews—Many of the Task Force volunteers staffed the phones and called what we thought were magnet schools in our area. Our conclusion as noted above about Deerfield's uniqueness stood out: many programs thought to be magnet schools were not; others were magnet programs as a subset of a school, and only a small handful were true magnet schools.

Our conclusion is that we have a unique educational offering providing choice to Novi's elementary aged families. The success of the program as measured by any means indicates that we should consider expansion of the magnet school program, not elimination.

As you can see by this proposal, it could not have been more comprehensive. Each point was backed up by pages of documentation. After hearing our parents present their documentation and proposal and then reading it over for myself, I don't know how one could not reach a conclusion in support of the merit of continuing Deerfield as a magnet school. There was so much evidence for the positive effect of magnet schools for a school district as well as the importance of choice for parents. The comment I heard from parents over and over was they felt their efforts were totally ignored and that they did not receive a credible answer from the school board in response to their proposal. They continually asked the question why, but never received a credible answer.

I felt ashamed for our school board on how they handled this. The one thing that a board member said at an open televised board meeting, which I heard repeated more times then I can count by our parents was that we had done too good a job. It reminds me of the quote from Frank Gifford, "People will forgive anything (stealing, killing, lying, etc.), but they won't forgive success." This pointed to the jealousy and contention in the district. I guess the question I would ask is how can someone do too good a job?

Our staff's commitment to Deerfield and what it represented in the quality of teaching and learning is reflected in the two letters on which staff collaborated and which were presented at a board meeting by Deerfield teachers Karen Swanson and Beverly Hatcher. This is very significant because staff was told by their teachers' association/union not to be vocal about their feelings because of possible repercussions. All present staff stood at the board meeting when these letters were read. It was a display of their tremendous passion and support for each other and what Deerfield stood for.

> Novi Community School District ... A
> Commitment to Excellence
> The district has invested a small fortune on motivational speakers over the years in an effort to inspire the staff. We've all heard about changing paradigms in education, been asked to "think out of the box," and been encouraged to build "learning communities" within our schools.

You may remember this quote from one of our beginning of the year speakers, "If you always do, what you've always done, you're always going to get, what you've always gotten."

Well, maybe that's what you want. This district has been good, maybe even great. But our commitment to excellence is what made us stand out as cutting edge and progressive; the place where people wanted to move and send their children to school. With our commitment to excellence, we've never been willing to say we are good enough!

Six years ago many of us were teaching in other elementary buildings in Novi. We were very happy. We were involved in wonderful cultures, and worked with fantastic teachers, parents, students, and administrators. But were drawn to the "vision" that Deerfield promised. We were asked to submit letters of interest, made to participate in the interview process, and required to sign papers stating that we were committed to that "vision." We then began the labor of love which created what we have today.

The Deerfield staff remains committed to our "vision." We thought it was your vision, too. Like our parents, we never imagined that you were no longer committed to offering a school of choice to the parents of Novi. We were shocked to hear that you would consider eliminating full-day kindergarten programs that have been successful, and the foundation of our K-4 program. Like our parents, we are disheartened and wonder why. We have never received any indication from the administration or the board, that we were not meeting the expectations of our commitment.

Please consider your commitment to excellence. What you decide tonight on the fate of Deerfield will send a strong message to the teachers, as to what you want for the future of the Novi Community School District. Please, don't make it easy for us to close our classroom doors, and do what has always been done.

Karen Swanson

February 9, 2006

To:	*Novi Community Schools Board of Education Members*
	Mr. Peter Dion, Superintendent
	Mrs. Nancy Davis, Assistant Superintendent

From:	*Beverly Hatcher, B.S., M.Ed.*

The parents and staff of Deerfield often speak of its culture, as what makes it unique. All Novi schools have a culture, but many people are uncertain what educators mean when they use the term. According to Webster's, culture is the application of labor or other means of improvement and the results of such efforts; it's the refinement of skills. I would like to address the culture of Deerfield.

Application of labor: The staff of Deerfield spent three weeks before the building opened to construct a multi-age curriculum that connected all of Novi's

Richard L. Njus

standards and benchmarks. Since all of our students would be learning in a K-4 setting, of which our full day kindergarten would be the foundation, we needed to shift the paradigm. We needed to rethink the way we had taught in the past. We needed to work as a team. We needed to have weekly grade level and house meetings. We needed to help one another, spend long hours after school, buy extra materials from our own resources, and have understanding families.

Improvement and Refinement of Skills: During the past six years, in order to enrich our culture, all of our skills have greatly improved. We not only understand but we apply differentiated instruction. During our staff meetings, we have created time to develop a professional learning community. Staff members share knowledge they have gained from conferences. We have had study groups to learn and apply multiple intelligence instruction and brain based learning. We have had book discussion groups and have read: Boyer's Basic School, Glasser's Choice Theory, Alfie Kohn's School's Children Deserve: Moving Beyond Traditional Classrooms and Tougher Standards, and Parker Palmer's Let Your Life Speak and The Courage to Teach. We are now in the process of studying The 17 Essential Qualities of a Team Player by John Maxwell. All of these activities have made us stronger, more creative teachers who are capable of integrating curriculum in flexible groups with the goal of developing independent, self-directed learners.

Results of such skills: I know you have the data

regarding our school. The parents of Deerfield, our partners in education, have done an outstanding job presenting the facts. Deerfield is, as measured by any standard, a success. In the beginning we were told Deerfield would continue if we could keep the school filled. Each year we have students waiting to attend at every grade level. We have students who love to learn. We have teachers who are excited to be stretched as educators. We have a principal filled with passion for our program. We have parents who volunteer countless hours.

Please continue Novi's commitment to excellence. Please consider these words of Elizabeth Dole's, "What you always do before you make a decision is consult. The best public policy is made when you are listening to the people who are going to be impacted." Please listen to our parents and students. Please listen to the Deerfield staff. Please let us continue our culture and keep Deerfield as a school of choice.

When these were read to the board, my heart swelled with pride for a staff who believed so strongly in their school that they were willing to stand together, placing themselves in possible jeopardy.

The board continued to receive hundreds of e-mails throughout the months of discussion, which gave even more credence to the desires of a large segment of the population they were voted to represent. Parents continued to attend school board meetings and speak on Deerfield's behalf and ask questions on the decisions of the school board. Parents who would never speak out in a confrontational way put themselves in an uncomfortable situation because of their passion for our school. The following letter is a great example of that:

> Appreciating Deerfield
>
> If you would have told me that one day I would stand before the local School Board to help in the fight to keep my children's elementary school's status intact, I would have said you were insane. Well, that's just where I found myself several times this past year. As the struggle to protect Deerfield's magnet school status carried on, community members who were never associated with Deerfield had a very difficult time understanding the reason for all of the commotion. Moreover, they couldn't see why these persistent parents wouldn't just let it go. I certainly can't speak for all of the other parents who were involved, but based on our family's personal experiences over the last three-and-a-half years at Deerfield, I can explain why we weren't willing to accept the decision without protest.
>
> Back in the spring of 2003, my husband and I struggled with the decision as to which elementary school would be the best fit for our oldest daughter. I must say we were thrilled that we lived in a school district that offered a choice. One evening our decision became clear after a conversation with a friend. You see, she had a child who was reading well above kindergarten level when he entered school. According to the teacher and principal at her son's school, the only extra stimulation they could offer her son was to

let him read occasionally to the class. We were so surprised to hear this. Prior to this conversation, we had toured Deerfield and done our homework regarding the teaching style there. We had heard that wonderful things were happening there like grouping children based on ability throughout various grades, thus offering students challenging opportunities to keep them from stagnating. This attribute of Deerfield all of a sudden became more attractive to us because it obviously wasn't going to be available everywhere. We didn't know if our children would be eligible for these opportunities, but the idea of them being available sure was comforting. All it took was that conversation to motivate us to pursue Deerfield for our children. Wouldn't you know, when our daughter entered kindergarten, she was given the option to go next door to the first/second-grade reading class along with some other classmates all year long. Had we made another choice, our daughter might have just been reading occasionally to her kindergarten class.

When our second child entered Deerfield two years later, our family's experience became even richer. The day our younger daughter started reading well in kindergarten, her teacher sent her over to her big sister's classroom two doors down so she could read to her. She was so excited and proud to be able to celebrate her success with her big sister. It was so heartwarming that the teacher was encouraging kids to be happy for one another and fostering sibling support.

These experiences I have mentioned so far might

never have been possible had it not been for the brilliant house concept. I can't say enough about the wonderful experiences our children and we as parents have had as a result of the K-4 grouping. It is fascinating how a building's layout can play such a major role in promoting the extraordinary bonds that develop between students, teachers, and parents. This feature of Deerfield alone is worthy of tremendous support.

In my opinion, the most impressive aspect of Deerfield is the phenomenal staff whose enthusiasm, dedication and creativity constantly amaze me. This staff, who live out the Deerfield pledge and expect the same from their students, creates that "caring community" providing an exceptional foundation for everything both in and out of the classroom. In addition, our family has been surprised on so many occasions by how teachers and other staff members have gone beyond our expectations to support or inspire our daughters. From the Spanish teacher suggesting resources to teach Dutch at home, to the writing teachers encouraging a young want-to-be author to keep journals and enter contests, and all in between, we are so grateful to them.

Of course, this staff couldn't do it without the unwavering support and guidance of their principal, Richard Njus. His passion and inspiration trickle down to his staff, and as a parent you can see that they are very motivated to be under his leadership. One of the finest illustrations of Mr. Njus's dedication occurred during our first year at Deerfield. He conducted a book study where parent participants read "The Shelter of Each Other" by Mary Pipher and met for several weeks in the evening to discuss it and share ideas. My husband and I were amazed that an elementary principal who lived an hour away would take the time to impress the importance of strong families upon his students' parents. This gave us the feeling that Deerfield's focus wasn't just on "the whole child," but rather on "the whole family." Over the years, we've discovered that that indeed is the case!

So you see, all the commotion, the speeches, the anxiety, the turmoil, etc. over the last year was all worth it to be able to be part of something bigger than just our children's elementary school. We always knew there was something extraordinary about Deerfield and the culture that has been created there. I guess we just had to be pushed to the edge to fully appreciate it and realize it was indeed worth fighting for.

Cheryl Roest

Staff, who put themselves in professional jeopardy, continued to write letters to the school board and spoke in support of the school. Parents went to the state superintendent of schools; the Michigan School Board Association, a national educational watchdog group; and even pursued lawsuits.

After months of meetings, e-mails, letters, articles in the newspaper, and countless hours of dialogue from parents to the district school board, in the spring of 2007, on a four-three vote, the board of education reconfirmed its decision for Deerfield to change to a neighborhood school. Deerfield would keep less than 140 of its 480 students, and the remaining students would be transferred to the other four elementary schools. Shortly after this decision was made, I received a note from Mrs. Elisabeth W. Bauer, one of our State Board of Education Members. She had visited Deerfield earlier that fall.

> Dear Mr. Njus,
> Thank you for taking time to welcome me to Deerfield Elementary School when Jane Hesse and I popped in on August 18. I was so excited to learn about the 3e connection [3e was the school in China that used concepts from Deerfield in their development] and the unique programming you have been doing. I was dismayed to learn from Jane later in the day that a local board decision will change the focus at Deerfield. It seems strange in an era where we need to be even more creative in our approaches to instruction. I hope you will continue to offer inspired and inspiring instruction to the children at Deerfield whether they arrive by choice or chance. You have them at a critical time in their learning experiences. Who they are when they leave you at age ten or so will greatly influence who they will become as adults. I will be thinking of you and your faculty and students and wishing you well.
>
> Mrs. Elizabeth W. Bauer, member
> Michigan State Board of Education

The note came for me at a perfect time. I needed the encouragement that we were doing what was right. It was also a confirmation that Deerfield was what we needed in public education today and that choice is what educators and parents recognized as a necessity in our society today. The note was also an encouragement to keep doing what we were doing in providing the best in inspired and inspiring instruction for our students.

Deerfield school had a very balanced representation of students from across the district. After redistricting, Deerfield would receive its students from the school closest to its building, which serviced the neighborhood around our building. When the final decision was made to redistrict, there was no overage in any of the schools in the school district. Deerfield was the only school in the district at capacity. The projections had distinctly changed for the school district because the economy had been strongly affected by the downturn of the automotive industry and the district had not grown as expected.

At Deerfield we knew that part of the lower increase in growth was due to the exiting parents unhappy with the school board's decision, who chose to move outside the district or back to private school. Another factor in the decline of enrollment was that parents from outside the district were not applying to come to Deerfield because of the board decision. As I said before, we usually would have twelve to twenty parents from outside the school district sign lease agreements for apartments, go through our lottery, and if they got into Deerfield, move into the district. The year the decision to redistrict was made making Deerfield a neighborhood school, we had no applicants with lease agreements when we held the lottery. Because of the change in the economy and decrease in enrollment of students, the school board was asked to reconsider redistricting until it was needed. Our parents suggested that if we redistricted then, we might have to redistrict again in the future if there was an imbalance in enrollment because of unforeseen growth in one area. They requested that the board use the time to reassess the merits of a magnet school and its benefit to the district. They also suggested studying the effectiveness of Deerfield's program.

Regretfully, the school board would not consider holding off on redistricting and moved ahead with their plan. Members of the board and administration admitted at board meetings that they did not have the overcrowding needed to redistrict at this time and did not foresee the need for the next year either. But they said it was a good time to do it. Their rationale was that it would open more opportunities to grandfather students to the school they were to leave. The bottom line when the figures came out for redistricting was that we would move 744 students to make Deerfield a neighborhood school. To say the least, this did not improve the contention throughout the district. The feelings of our parents can be summed up by poem by Karen Abraham:

Restructuring tries to make the change
Only brings frustration and rage
At a system that doesn't see
All the good that we can be
Takes us for granted

Disenchanted
Exhausted
Grieving
Sad
Think of leaving
And I could
Maybe,
I
Should

All these thoughts ran through my mind and the minds of staff and parents. I had many parents tell me they were afraid to mention that they were from Deerfield when they were with neighbors, at community functions, or social engagements for fear of the reaction they would receive. Some parents shared that they had lost friendships over the issues surrounding Deerfield. It was one of the most heart-wrenching experiences I have ever gone through.

The question that everyone kept asking was *why*. This was so baffling. Those to whom I spoke from outside our school district could not understand the board's decision. I had many conversations with administrators about that decision. It was said and inferred by many upper administration and school board members in conversations that the board had made a mistake. Remember it was a four-three vote. If they had made a mistake, then why didn't they take a step back and review their decision. Every time I asked about this, I was given the answer: "We can't look back; we have to move on." Why? Why was it so hard to say that we made a mistake or just that we want to table this for more review?

True leaders admit when they are wrong. In speaking on why Gandhi held such personal power in his nonviolent work in India, Martin Luther King Jr. referred to Gandhi's ability to make his will sincere. As quoted earlier in this text:

> If you ask people in India why is it that Mahatma Gandhi was able to do what he did in India, they will say they followed him because of his absolute sincerity… Any time he made a mistake, even in his personal life, or even a decision that he made in the independence struggle, he came out in public and said, "I made a mistake."

Why is that so hard? We need to stay open and be sincere, which involves accepting that we will falter and need a course correction. Confucius speaks of this when he says, "Making the will sincere is allowing for no self-deception." I think the board would have established a great amount of credibility if they would have stepped back and reviewed their decision. We need to expand our thinking. It goes along with Einstein's notion that "you can't solve a problem by the thinking that created it." It goes along with the question I continued to ask, what do we want for our school district? It needed to be rethought.

To emphasize this I will relay a conversation I had with Quentin Messer, Jr., Vice President of Development for Edison Schools. He came to visit me to discuss the possibility of starting a charter school because of his conversations with parents from Deerfield, who considered forming a local charter school to replicate Deerfield. During our two and one half hour conversation and tour of our school, he many times asked me *why*. He was extremely impressed with the quality of our programming and the engagement of our students in learning. He said why would a school board dismantle a program like this? He went on to say that superintendents around the country would do anything to have a gem like Deerfield to showcase their school district. It was affirming for me to hear this about our school, but also very disheartening.

From the time the board made the decision on Deerfield, my time was consumed by parents on this issue. This was not negative. I wanted to help them deal with their questions, grief, and anger. The strength of the family culture of this school was evident. Parents were incredibly vested in the school, not to speak of their children. There was such a sense of *our* school, an ownership, a deep feeling of family. It was a culture of *we*.

One example of this ownership is a conversation I had with a couple after their parent-teacher conference for their twin kindergarten boys. They had only been in our school nine weeks, and they talked about how significantly their sons had been affected by their experience in Deerfield. They said their one son the year before would not go to preschool. This year he wouldn't leave school for a doctor's appointment because he loved school so much. Both boys progressed very quickly academically. The father said it was not the curriculum or building, it was the culture that made the difference. He then went on to tell me that his neighbor got in the lottery for their first-grade child and took a space at Deerfield knowing they would have to leave after a year because of redistricting. They wanted their child to have at least one year of the Deerfield experience. That was heart warming, but at the same time, saddening.

I had daily discussions with parents after the decision to redistrict was finalized about what they were going to do when redistricted. Many were considering moving to private and charter schools. There was even a committee pursuing the creation of a charter school in our school district. The grief, anxiety, frustration, and anger of parents who were being uprooted from a school they loved and in which they were so vested was intense and heart wrenching. It was communicated in the eyes and reactions of parents when we talked about the future. I remember one day when a mother was volunteering and brought her toddler along. I was having fun with him and talking to her about him, and she said, "Wait until you get ... " and then she stopped with a sad look on her face. Her family would not be in the school the next year. How does one deal with something like that?

It is so difficult to describe the sense of helplessness in this situation. The feeling is that there is no credible reason for redistricting, and that there is no valid reason to dismantle a program, which so much effort had gone into to create, without considerable study. Even more, the success of the program is very evident. For me, the principal, I found it very difficult to support the party line of the district with the tremendous investment I made in the school and with my own stand on our school and the tremendous value it has for students. For seven years it had been a realized dream that sadly turned into a nightmare. I feel sometimes in public education we are our own worst enemies. We shoot ourselves in the foot. When a school finds a high level of success, the questions begin to arise. Then begins the jealousy, complaints, and comparisons. This creates a difficult position for those who are in power and their ability to answer the questions honestly without raising concern for others. I have experienced this over the years; one works with staff and parents to create an innovative, forward-moving school, and the stones start to come. Again, as Dr. Parker Palmer said in the beginning of our second year at Deerfield, "You are a satellite and they will try to pull you back into traditionalism."

Education must change to meet the needs of students going into a much different world from the one we started in. We have to create a young person who can compete and live in an international society, a person who accepts diversity and embraces change. Our schools should not look like they did when we went to school. If we don't address this, who will? We need to be true to ourselves. We know we need significant change. I like the way the Jewish Elder Hillel puts it, "If I am not myself, who will be? And when I am myself, what am I? And if not now, when?" Now is the time to address what is best for kids.

The dynamics in the district changed dramatically after the decision on redistricting. For five years Deerfield was a showcase for visitors. I continually had calls from our district superintendent for tours of people visiting from outside the district. Then when the decision was made to make us a neighborhood school, Deerfield was, as a colleague said, "pushed off the plate." We became the ugly stepsister. We felt as if we were placed in a vacuum. Deerfield was not mentioned at meetings, or if mentioned, the responses to comments about Deerfield were met with silence or challenge. Staff commented frequently on how they felt shunned by colleagues from other schools in the district when at district meetings. Staff also shared negative comments that administrators made at these meetings about Deerfield. One comment that came back to me was, "We don't want to hear about what you are doing at Deerfield." This was very demoralizing to staff. There was also significant tension between the other elementary principals and me. It was as if they reasoned if we ignore them, maybe they will go away.

On February 9, 2006, the district school board met at Deerfield as they do in all school buildings throughout the year. My staff prepared an outstanding PowerPoint presentation for the meeting. I started by having my staff introduce themselves. Then I introduced the co-presidents of our parent council to speak and introduce the rest of our parent board. Our presidents were very complimentary of our staff and what their involvement in Deerfield had done for their families. It was great for our staff to hear. Two of our staff members presented to the board. They did an outstanding job. It could have not been better. It truly grasped the essence of our school. I then spoke and showed a video. After I showed the video, I asked the board if there were any questions.

Normally there would be questions and/or comments from every board member. They usually compliment the staff on the outstanding job they are doing. There was silence. Then the superintendent spoke, thanking the teachers who spoke, not our parents or me. Then the board president haltingly spoke, and another board member said his grandchildren had a good experience here. But he also voted against the magnet school issue. The previous month at another school, after their presentation, the school board gushed over the presentation by the staff. The board's silence spoke volumes. I think I can best sum it up by two e-mails—one from our parent group president and another by a very supportive parent, which were sent to the board after the meeting.

Dear Board Members,

Over the course of the past year, I have addressed you on several occasions regarding my concerns over redistricting. I have tried to convey my disappointment and my questions to you in a professional manner. I have been careful not to attack personally (unless I was attacked first) or call in to question your integrity. In part because that is not my style, but also because I recognize that you are volunteers giving your time to our community. However, I must convey my disbelief, dismay, and just plain anger with this Board over the lack of real support or affirmation given toward the Deerfield staff after the incredible presentation that they put on tonight. We had Ms. Elfring's very weak thank you, that as president she was obliged to make, and Mr. Brown's comments about his grandchildren attending Deerfield and how well loved they were. I was shocked beyond words that these were the only comments from this Board. Especially in light of the glowing comments made at Novi Woods during the December 7th Board Meeting. I remember comments like, "If we could bottle this and sell it, we would be millionaires." I realize that many of the Deerfield parents have been very, very critical of this Board; however, that is no reason to be so utterly dismissive and completely unsupportive of the Deerfield staff. I find it difficult to believe that you couldn't muster any questions or anything supportive to say. Here's a suggestion: "That was a wonderful presentation. Thank you, Deerfield staff, for all you do." This utter lack of sensitivity and your continued refusal to acknowledge the concerns of parents and staff at Deerfield is exactly what is driving so much of the criticism of this Board. I believe each of you owes the staff at Deerfield a heartfelt apology; however, I won't hold my breath.

Sincerely,
Kim Love
President, Deerfield Community Council

Dear School Board Members:

I am sure you have heard from several parents about our disappointment in the lack of feedback from the board about our school and the presentation they so carefully prepared for the board meeting on Thursday evening.

Having been at every other elementary school for their presentation to the board, except Parkview, I am also struggling to understand the reluctance of this board to acknowledge their efforts. Why is it okay to admire and praise the efforts of the other schools, but offer so little acknowledgment when it comes to Deerfield? It would almost appear that it has now become politically incorrect to say anything in favor of Deerfield because there is a fear of offending the other elementary schools. It is incredibly unfortunate that acknowledging those who stepped out in faith six and a half years ago, achieved all that this district asked of them, and continue to provide 480 children from this district with a quality education in spite of the lack of support from their peers in this district (and will be losing the support of many of the families that have supported, encouraged and acknowledged their efforts) is viewed as negative comment about the other schools. It has absolutely nothing to do with those other schools, and failing to give them their due, you endorsed the idea that it does.

As I sat through all the other presentations, I was impressed by the enthusiasm of the teachers at Village Oaks and the way they are encouraged to explore and create environments for learning that are uniquely their own. I was thrilled to see how Orchard Hills is engaging students at every level with their reading program. At Novi Woods I was encouraged to see the cooperative efforts among the staff to address all children's learning needs. Not once in the course of their presentations did I feel that anything they presented cast my children's elementary school in an unfavorable light. Each school is clearly different and marked with a culture that is uniquely its own. I do not doubt that they are all wonderful schools. Deerfield is a wonderful school as well. Your failure to acknowledge that publicly is not only unfortunate, but it continues to

Richard L. Njus

perpetuate the negative sentiment has been prevalent in this district of late.

Somehow we need to stop this cycle. Choosing or endorsing Deerfield is not a reflection on any other school. It is somewhat like requesting one teacher over another because of your child's particular personality or learning style. It is not a reflection on any other teacher, but a desire for your child to have a teacher whose philosophy and style of teaching is consistent with his particular learning needs. (Deerfield has been a good fit for many, but not for all.) Some parents have even opted to send their children to different elementary schools in an effort to accommodate this. The inability to accommodate the desire for this program is something that has needed to be addressed for some time, and it is certainly within this district's ability to do so. It also will within this districts ability to put an end to the anti-Deerfield sentiment that continues to plague our community. (Think Committee to Unite Novi.)

We have excellent teachers across this district. With four children (one at each school level), I have had quite a cross-section of teachers. I am continually amazed by their commitment and enthusiasm, their view of this role, not just as a job, but as a calling, and their efforts to improve educational delivery and explore different teaching methods. I am currently participating in the School Day committee at the high school, and can't begin to tell you how impressed I am by the dedication of the teachers I have met through that experience. I am certain that these same teachers are able to rise above the current sensitive political climate given an adequate model to follow.

We also have intelligent, informed parents in this community who I am confident can also rise above the prevailing attitude, given the encouragement and the impetus to do so. It is in within each one of you to provide that. "Success, real success, in any endeavor demands more from an individual than most people are willing to offer not more than they are capable of offering," James Roche (from the Novi Meadows Dec. 15th newsletter).

This is an awesome district, but the ability of this district to stay at the top of the game is in the hands of those that lead—this School Board and Administration.

"If your actions inspire others to dream more, learn more, do more, and become more, you are a leader." John Quincy Adams as quoted by Dr. Falls in his November 10th newsletter.

Do any of you honestly believe that succumbing to the negative sentiment in this community has inspired anyone?

The staff at Deerfield deserved more than a cursory acknowledgment, and I hope some of you will see fit to publicly correct your error. It is truly never too late to do the right thing.

Sincerely,
Bobbie Murphy

To say the least, I spent the next few days encouraging staff and parents who had been hurt, let down, just generally demoralized. There was a sense of hollowness. Staff commented, "Are we on an island and they would like us to just go away?" Trust has so much importance in the attitude of staff. They had lost their trust in the school board and the superintendent. And unfortunately our students were starting to hear and feel the change that was coming.

My journey to Deerfield began before the school even had a name! As a Novi teacher, I volunteered to be a part of "The Innovative Elementary Program" cadre. We held our first meeting in April, 1997, a full three years before the school opened. Our charge was to research the best practices in education, to visit schools of choice and charter schools, and to report back to the cadre. We then disaggregated all of our data and from that decided what would be the best path to follow at our new innovative elementary school.

The Novi Community School Board told the teachers and principal, who interviewed and were selected to be a part of Deerfield, that the school of choice would continue as long as we were able to keep it full and our test scores were competitive with the rest of the district. The first year, we had two empty $3^{rd}/4^{th}$-grade classrooms. However, after the first year we had student waiting lists at all grade levels. Parents were even willing to transfer their children mid-year if an opening occurred. And our test scores have met or exceeded the rest of the district!

In fact, in Deerfield's final year as a school of choice, we far exceeded the other schools.

Our school did not develop into the positive learning environment it has become without a great deal of hard work, long hours, stress, co-operation, team building, and parent involvement. During the first year, when I headed home after spending long hours after school planning with my partners, I often wondered, "What have I done?" Our school had very few materials and we were constantly creating activities for our students. Since we were working in a multi-age setting, we also needed to develop a cohesive curriculum. Various staff members worked together to create and share what we needed. We all offered help when our areas of expertise applied. We applauded one another's hard work and appreciated the "sharing" atmosphere.

I can't help but find it ironic that although we spent three years planning Deerfield, it was dismantled in less than six months. I still do not have a clear understanding of why Deerfield is no longer a school of choice. Parents, students, and staff members presented a great deal of data that was simply ignored. Surprisingly, one board member (at a meeting) stated that we at Deerfield had done "too good a job." I wondered.... do you mean that too many people want to be at Deerfield and it's causing problems? If so, why not continue to be forward thinking and create another school of choice? Instead, our district decided to take a giant step backwards. At a time when other districts are looking for ways to keep parents in public education, ours has figured out a way to make our families want to leave!

Now we have to move on … we'll grieve the loss of the students & parents who are not in our designated home school boundaries. However, we'll persevere and, once again, work as a cohesive group to welcome our new Deerfield families.

Opinion of: Beverly Hatcher, 1–2 Teacher

"I love this school and I don't want everything to change.
My family is sad because we are moving in the summer.
I don't want things to change."

Gabby, first grader

Chapter 12

Bitter or Better

"What we have once enjoyed we can never lose.
All that we love deeply becomes a part of us."

Helen Keller

The Deerfield story is not over. The dream will survive. Deerfield will continue on as a school, and those who are leaving to go to another school or move away are still a part of the Deerfield family. How does one move from an experience where the connections run so deep, where lives are so intertwined, and so many questions are still unanswered? I had hundreds of discussions with parents over the two years prior to the redistricting about all the issues of changing Deerfield from a magnet school to a neighborhood school. The closer we came to the change and movement of students from Deerfield, the more the conversation turned to what will we do now. Many feelings of anger, grief, and loss were expressed by parents and staff who felt that there were many questions left unanswered.

The major question for me was what do we take from this experience? Does one go away from such a significant experience better or bitter? The more I thought on this, and the more parents, staff, and I shared, the more I saw a need for healing. I felt a need for centering in on what we all take from the experience, whether we stay or go. I wanted all of us to be better not bitter.

I said at our final district school board meeting at Deerfield before the change from a magnet school to a neighborhood school that it was my hope that our students would not only take their head knowledge, but their heart knowledge; that they would represent Deerfield through their respect, responsibility, and care wherever they go. That was most important.

All our questions may not be answered, but we needed to move forward with our lives. In life, many times we have questions that aren't answered until years down the line. While on a flight to Florida, I was reading the book *Spiritual Direction, Wisdom for the Long Walk of Faith*, by one of my favorite authors, Henri Nouwen. He used a quote by Rainer Maria Rilke that spoke to me about this quandary of unanswered questions.

> I want to beg you as much as I can ... to be patient toward all that is unsolved in your heart and to try to love the questions themselves ... Do not now seek answers which cannot be given you because you would not be able to live them. And the point is to live everything. Live the questions now. Perhaps you will then gradually, without noticing it, live along some distant day into the answer ... Take whatever comes with great trust, and if only it comes out of your will, out of some need of your innermost being, take it upon yourself and hate nothing.

What a strong statement.

When we don't have answers to questions, we need to keep moving forward, because in distant days we may live into the answer. I encouraged parents and staff as we looked to the future, no matter what happened, that we needed to move forward without hate, with a sense of purpose, with a sense of the richness of our experience; to be better, not bitter; to take to our next experience the richness of what we had learned together. As I reflected over the two-year struggle over Deerfield, I felt that the Deerfield experience had the richness to set the tone for the rest of our lives; that it would add significance to what we would experience from then on.

My wish whether staying or leaving Deerfield was that we, staff, parents, and students, keep the heart of our culture as an essential part of our lives. Wherever we go, to take the experience of what deep connections to others and a purpose can mean to lives; to be the force for that kind of deep experience in other schools and organizations through an openness and willingness to take risks and connect. If we are better not bitter, we would take into our world what is best, and we would all make a difference for good.

The culture of Deerfield, that living core of beliefs that runs through our organization and lives, became a part of us and cannot be taken away. This was summed up nicely in an illustration one of our student teachers used in a thank you note to me at the completion of her student teaching assignment.

Dear Mr. Njus,

This is just a small note to thank you for allowing me to learn and grow as an educator. I feel so lucky to have been part of such a wonderful school. Deerfield is truly a unique educational setting. From day one, I could sense the caring, supportive community you, the teachers, parents, and staff work so hard to create. Just as children benefit from learning in a nurturing, supportive, compassionate environment, I too have gained from my time at Deerfield Elementary School. I wish you all the luck in the future and know that even though things are scheduled to change at Deerfield next year, from what I have observed and learned over the past few months, I am confident Deerfield itself will not change. Your current situation reminds me of a great oak tree in the middle of the woods. You can change the environment around the tree, build houses, add roads, and even a Wal-Mart, but that oak tree will never change; its core essence will always be just what it is—an oak tree. I believe Deerfield will continue to be Deerfield, because just like the tree in the woods, your teachers, community, and your combined beliefs are strong and unbreakable!

Many thanks,

Amy Santi
Elementary Education Student
Teacher, Madonna University

I like the comparison with a strong oak tree. Amy's last phrase sums up the culture of Deerfield, the combined beliefs which are strong and unbreakable. It is how I defined culture earlier in this book. Culture is the living core beliefs that run through the texture of an organization. It is the heartbeat of an organization.

As you have read throughout these pages, Deerfield is a special place which touched hearts and challenged minds in a rich way. I have heard over and over how students' experiences at Deerfield turned around and changed their lives. I shared a few of those stories in this book. Jonathan Byrnes wrote in a Harvard Business School publication: "The ultimate reward is the deep satisfaction that comes from seeing something new that wouldn't have been there if you had not created it." The Deerfield family needed to reflect on and celebrate the special rich experience we had in creating our school and the reward of being a part of something new that wouldn't have been if we hadn't put our heads and hearts together to do it. How can one walk away bitter from that? We lived through a special experience. We were a part of a school that took on a personality of wonder, a heart of care, and a vision for success for all students.

Are we the only school in the country in which this has happened? No. There are schools and pockets of this going on all over the United States. Two schools I know of as good examples are Key School in Indianapolis, Indiana, a kindergarten-through-twelfth-grade public magnet school; and Winnwood Elementary, a kindergarten-through-fifth-grade public school that follows the Basic School Framework in north Kansas City, Kansas. Both of these schools are located in the inner city in a low-income area and are an oasis for quality learning. Walking into those schools you feel the energy of their culture for learning. They were created with people who put their heads and hearts together and through determination and hard work proved the world wrong. Inner-city schools can thrive, and their students can experience the richness of learning. We need to learn from them and apply the attributes of their successes to all schools. There are years of research to draw from to direct us in this endeavor.

In my more than thirty years in education, the experience of the last seven years has touched my life in a richer way than any other school I have served. That is not to say I haven't worked in some great schools with outstanding staffs. I have. What made the difference at Deerfield was putting together a researched program of best practices in teaching and learning that met the learning needs of all students; a staff committed to the program and meeting all student needs; and parents who chose to be in the school and true partners with the school and involved in their child's learning. This culminated in a very unique and rich culture for learning. I have always said, "If a child can connect with one teacher in her or his learning experience, it can make all the difference in his or her life." Our teachers were connectors; that has made a huge difference at Deerfield.

I shared in the first chapter of this book the difference one teacher who connected with me made in my life. It made all the difference in the world. It has made me the person I am, the person who can pass that connection on to others. I go back to Frederick Bueckner's quote, "Where the passion of your heart meets the needs of the world, this is your joy."

My passion is kids. The joy is seeing them successful and full of the joy of learning. Kids connect with that.

What do I want the Deerfield family to take from our experiences? What do I want everyone to take from this experience? I want us to take our joy of learning, our heart of care, and our understanding of others, which is so needed in this world. We need our "caring community of learners" to connect with others to be successful peacemakers in an international society.

And, we who stayed at Deerfield with the changes or for those who left with their changes, it is important to keep the fire of the special culture of care and learning burning brightly in our hearts. To the question bitter or better; may we go from Deerfield better having proven the essence and purpose of what Deerfield was all about. Those who stay, stay with the purpose to love every child who comes through the doors, to connect with them and strive to make Deerfield better than it has ever been.

Wherever we go, we should strive to create a school that makes a difference. A parent from Deerfield sent me the following quote by Picasso, which I feel embodies the kinds of schools we need to create:

> Each second we live is a new and unique moment of the universe, a moment that will never be again. And what do we teach our children? We teach them that two and two make four, and that Paris is the capital of France. When will we also teach them what they are? We should say to each of them: Do you know what you are? You are a marvel. You are unique. In

all the years that have passed, there has never been another child like you. Your legs, your arms, your clever fingers, the way you move. You may become a Shakespeare, a Michelangelo, a Beethoven. You have the capacity for anything. Yes, you are a marvel. And when you grow up, can you then harm another who is, like you, a marvel? You must work, we must all work, to make the world worthy of its children.

What a wonderful definition of what a school should be about. I hope the Deerfield experience for all of our students has helped them learn to their potential, but even more, that they realized they are all unique, special, a marvel. They have the capacity to do anything, prove the world wrong, and that they will all grow up to make the world a better place for their children.

We are all different from the experience of Deerfield. I never in my wildest dreams thought we would create a place like it. I know I am different from the person I was in 1999. I personally do not hold any grudges or anger. I admit I do get frustrated. But the last two years have given me the wonderful opportunity to see and experience the depth of the culture we created. It has helped me feel and know that when people put their heads and hearts together, they can make a tremendous difference. And I have also learned without a shadow of a doubt that the connections and intensity of the Deerfield experience can happen anywhere, in any school, if people so desire and are willing to give of themselves to make it happen.

Richard L. Njus

As I think of the future for those who experienced Deerfield and all who are involved in schools, I encourage all parents and teachers to take risks, follow their hearts, and prove the world wrong. Wherever you go in your next school as a student, parent, or a teacher, be a part of making it the best. Do not accept mediocrity. Children need us as their role models and examples to help them experience and capture the joy of learning. As parents and teachers, we are competing with television, video games, and other distractions that keep our children from fulfilling their greatest potential. We can be the igniters of our children's love of learning and help them expand their view of the world. We can help them see the unlimited opportunities they have through their education. We want to develop the whole child: mind, heart, and soul.

This brings me to a final quote from Dr. Ernest L. Boyer, "I know how idealistic it may sound, but it is my urgent hope that in the century ahead students in the nation's schools will be judged not by their performance on a single test but by the quality of their lives. It's my hope that students in the classrooms of tomorrow will be encouraged to be creative, not conforming, learning to cooperate rather than compete." I hope as Boyer did that Deerfield and all schools will encourage students to be creative, cooperative, caring, and full of the joy of learning. Our students should be judged not by grades, but by the quality of their lives.

Thursday, March 13, 2008
Dear Mr. Njus,
My husband and I wanted to share some of our thoughts and experiences with you on how our first

year has been here at Deerfield as we head toward the last few months of the school year.

It was just about a year ago when my husband and I met with you in your office to discuss whether or not our daughter should move over to Deerfield from her former elementary school due to the redistricting that was to be taking place in the Novi Schools. We informed you that our daughter suffers from a condition referred to as Selective Mutism (SM). SM is a social anxiety disorder that affects children, primarily in a school setting. These children (and sometimes young adults) cope with their anxiety by becoming mute when placed in an environment that is perceived as frightening or threatening. You reassured my husband and me that our daughter would be loved at Deerfield whether or not she would be able to become verbal during her elementary years.

Before attending Deerfield Elementary, our daughter had been mute (with both teachers and children) in the four previous years she had spent in school. She was mute in preschool for two years, and she was also mute in kindergarten and first grade in her former elementary school in Novi. It has been very trying and emotional for my husband and me to watch our daughter suffer so badly in silence in school.

We really did not expect things to be much different this school year when our daughter first started attending Deerfield last August. I was excited about the school being so beautiful, and so close to our home, but never did I think she would begin to speak to anyone at school.

Wow, we have been thrilled with the social and verbal progress our daughter has been making this year! There have been gradual, but progressive steps throughout this year. She speaks with other children in the building. She has actually read in front of her teacher. She even raised her hand in class to give a correct answer out loud in front of her classmates. I realize that most parents who are lucky enough to not have a child, who has an issue, or a special need, may think I'm crazy. This has just uplifted our spirits beyond words.

We truly believe the environment that she is in at Deerfield has helped to lower our daughter's anxiety in school. She feels so comfortable with the "house" concept. The multi-age classroom has been such a great confidence builder for her. She just loves it when she thinks she is helping another classmate out. Of course, you and your entire staff are the core of why this has worked out so well. Having a staff that have been informed and educated about SM is wonderful. Mrs. Griesinger, and Mrs. Semeyn, in the Birdhouse, actually deserve "dual teachers of the year" in the NCSD. They have made her feel so relaxed and comfortable in their classroom. The fact that our daughter was able to speak in that classroom at her still very young age, suffering from SM, is just miraculous.

I did also want to mention that I continue to meet regularly with many parents in Southeastern Michigan (and also nationally) who also have children suffering from SM. Hundreds of these children still have not uttered a word in school, many of them are older than my daughter. My husband and I feel pretty lucky. The best thing about what has been happening this year is that our daughter is so happy!

Thanks to All of You So Much,
New Deerfield Parent

Richard L. Njus

Chapter 13

Looking to the Future

"Education is not the filling of a pail,
but the lighting of a fire."

William Butler Yeats

To conclude, Deerfield was a magnet school focused on pushing educational boundaries and providing a culture conducive to learning that would engage students. Deerfield's program was built on tried and proven best practices in teaching learning. We experienced great success as seen through our test scores, parent approval, and most importantly, in our students. But we can not set back our on our laurels. We must continue the process of development and revision of our program. We need to ask ourselves, what does the future hold for our kids? And what do our schools need to do to prepare them for their future? We need to prepare our children to live in a global, virtual world. If you have read *The World Is Flat* by Thomas K. Friedman, you can see how rapidly our world is changing and how dramatically the landscape of business and industry is developing throughout the world. The students of tomorrow have to be prepared to work and live anywhere in the world. We talk about being global, but we don't live it out in our approach to teaching. At Deerfield we have to continue to work on changing our mindset and to start acting globally. Dr. Yong Zhao, a professor from Michigan State University, said at a conference on international education that we need to think, *Every child, every day in an international society.* Children from an early age need to be taught to think globally. Their world will be much different from ours. The talents of the world won't be centered in the United States; we will have a global trade of talents. This can be further emphasized through the opening paragraph of the introduction of the book *A Whole New Mind Moving from the Information Age to the Conceptual Age*, by Daniel H. Pink.

> The last few decades have belonged to a certain kind of person with a certain kind of mind—computer programmers who could crank code, lawyers who could craft contracts, MBAs who could crunch numbers. But the keys to the kingdom are changing hands. The future belongs to a very different kind of person with a very different kind of mind—creators and empathizers, pattern recognizers, and meaning makers. These people—artists, inventors, designers, reap society's richest rewards and share its greatest joys.

We see some of this happening today. Think of the outsourcing of work throughout the world. The work goes where the inexpensive skills are. Just look at the professionals you interact with and where they received their training and their country of origin.

What talents will the U.S. have to offer to the world in the future? What will our children need to know? Herbert

Spencer said in 1859, "What knowledge is of most worth?" We need to keep asking ourselves this question: Is everything we are teaching students of benefit? This kind of thinking breaks one out of traditionalism into futuristic thinking about learning. The best thing we can do is to teach our students to be learners. Education needs to light the fire of learning. We cannot teach a body of knowledge; it is multiplying too rapidly. Students need to know how to learn. They need to know how to access information to use and learn. In this virtual world, our children can go anywhere and access information. With this unlimited access to the world, we need to teach character in a virtual world. It is character development of respect, responsibility, and caring, which will help students in their life choices. It is the building of personal integrity. This starts with our youngest and is reinforced all the way through school.

In the *World Is Flat*, Friedman says there are three keys for the future, the three Ts: technology, talent, tolerance. Character development is a way of life modeled in the home and school where children respect and celebrate differences. It enables us to move seamlessly from country and culture to country and culture. We need to model and instill this in our children. As Muhatma Gandhi said, "There is only one race—the human race." It is not us and them, it is all of us. We worked with this at Deerfield. We stressed respect, responsibility, and caring through our pledge, international festival, and the flags of countries in our cafeteria. We did it in the classroom, in conversation, and we infused it in our curriculum. One of our staff developed a language arts program taking books from writers around the world to teach the genre for literature. It was also a great tool for teaching about other cultures and ignited outstanding conversations in our classes. We need to continue to do more in this area.

We as adults need to model what we want for our students. We try to live and work with a global view. Mezzo-soprano Marian Anderson, the first black Metropolitan Opera singer, said, "There are many persons ready to do what is right because in their hearts they know it is right. But they hesitate, waiting for the other fellow to make the first move—and he, in turn, waits for you." At Deerfield we tried to model and teach our students to take the first step.

When we think of the process of teaching and learning to meet the challenge of the future, we need to think of our students as Picasso says, "All children are born artists, the problem is to remain an artist as they grow up." In society and in education, we tend to layer over our children with our expectations so much so that they don't know themselves and their art. Sometimes schooling gets in the way of education. "I have never let my schooling interfere with my education," said Mark Twain. We have to be careful as educators that our structure, curriculum, and programs do not inhibit the learner from reaching their greatest potential. At Deerfield we did this by emphasizing the joy of learning.

Education is moving from an emphasis on the left brain to an emphasis on the right brain. In an article in *Phi Delta Kappa International*, "Education in the Flat World," Dr. Yong Zhao talked about creativity as the most important, sought after commodity in the twenty-first century. Creativity leads to innovation in every area. Many times our students are educated out of creativity through tests and regulations. Sir

Richard L. Njus

Ken Robinson defined creativity as "the process of having original ideas that have value." How many times have you and I seen an original idea squelched in a school? It doesn't go along with the lesson plan or the way we are supposed to learn something. I can see the look on kids' faces when this has happened. They had a light bulb go on, and we turn it off. We need to value the richness of human capacity, the gift of human imagination. Sir Ken Robinson in a video said the following:

> We need to see our creative capacity for the richness they are, and seeing children for the hope they are. Our job is to educate their whole being so they can face their future.
>
> We may not see the future, but they will. Our job is to help them make something of it.

That pretty well sums it up. We need an education for the whole person. Students need to know themselves. At Deerfield we developed programs which help students discover themselves through identification of their multiple-intelligences and their personalities through an instrument such as True Colors. It is fascinating to see how perceptive and understanding of others children are when they understand personalities.

When we look at the educational framework in our schools and the demands of the future, they may all have to change. Our schools should not look like the ones we attended. In Dr. Yong Zhao's article, "Education in the Flat World," he said,

Left-brain, sequential, literal, functional, textual, and analytic thinking is no longer sufficient. As we move into the Conceptual Age, what really matters is right—brain, simultaneous, metaphorical, aesthetic, contextual, and synthetic thinking—the type that is not assessed well on standardized tests.

We need to increase our curriculum for study in science and technology. Our schools need to be dual language. We need to start teaching world languages in preschool through high school. It not only helps us to communicate with our world family but to understand them.

To develop the schools for tomorrow we should study other countries' educational systems. What is successful and why. We don't need to reinvent the wheel. We need to collaborate and share our intelligence. I remember talking to educators in China. They do well in math and science, and the U.S. does well in literacy and the affective domain for learning. How do we take the best from each experience in learning to make us both better? We have a wealth of knowledge on learning; we just need to share it for the betterment of the whole world society. We have to think globally.

Our educational system should educate the whole child with a strong basic education rich in literacy, science, and math. It should encourage and nurture creativity and celebrate individuality and diversity.

This will cause us to change not only our mindset but our practices. We have to look at what we teach, define what we need to teach, and change. Training will be key to bring staff onboard in this challenge. We will all have to change our thinking on how we will live and learn globally. Will it be easy? No. But it is imperative for our children's future. It is a substantial investment in our school and our children. We will reap tremendous benefits and rewards. It goes back to a statement I shared earlier from Charles Swindoll, "We are all faced with a series of great opportunities brilliantly disguised as impossible situations." I also go back to the statement that I have used frequently in this book. When people put their heads and hearts together, they will create something very special. We realized this at Deerfield, but we also need to put our heads and hearts together across the world and create schools for success for our human race. Our children are our future. They are worth whatever it takes, and nothing should stand in our way of helping them be the best they can be. That was our desire at Deerfield, to enrich the lives of all children and their families.

In closing, I would like to thank every parent, teacher, and staff member who put faith in me and richly touched my life. And to my kids, our students and my joy, I would like from the bottom of my heart to thank you for sharing your life with me, for your hugs, and all that you did to make me feel special as your principal. I wish for you all the greatest success and blessings this world can bring. I encourage you to follow your hearts, because where the passion of your heart is, there you will find your joy. Prove the world wrong. Carry the light of Deerfield in your heart; Deerfield is a special place because of those who entered its doors and left better for their experience. They will be able to take their place in our international society with minds and hearts that will make a difference for good.

I would like to end with the quote that is posted outside the main office at our school. May you all be a masterpiece.

Painting or Masterpiece?
We are born into the world like a blank canvas,
and each person that crosses our path takes
up the brush and makes his mark upon our surface.
So it is that we develop.
But we must realize that there comes a day that we
Must take up the brush and finish the work.
For only we can decide if we are to be just another
painting or a masterpiece.

—Unknown

Richard L. Njus